S0-DRJ-997

JAL
Guide to
the People's
Republic
of China

毛主席菩薩蠻大柏地詞意　乾石

JAL
Guide to the People's Republic of China

Arne J. de Keijzer with Fredric M. Kaplan

Eurasia
Press

Fair Lawn, New Jersey

FIRST EDITION

Typography by U.S. Lithograph Inc.
Calligraphy by David Ta-chun Lin
Cover design and cartography by Ellen Glass
Book design by Kathie Brown

ISBN: 0-932030-01-7
LIBRARY OF CONGRESS
CATALOG CARD NUMBER 78-58817

Printed in the United States of America

CONTENTS

THE CHINA ITINERARY **51**

GUIDE TO THE CHINESE EXPORT COMMODITIES FAIR ("CANTON FAIR") **193**

INDEX TO CITIES
AND MAJOR SITES

MAPS

TABLES AND CHARTS

INTRODUCTION

As this book was being prepared, China travel was undergoing a revolution. Indeed, as recently as the mid-1970s, there were few places on earth less accessible to the Western tourist than China. In 1977, however, China travel officials began to re-examine the policies that had for nearly three decades kept the country off limits to all but a select group of specialists, traders, and sympathetic observers. By early 1978, China began to welcome the first of what promised to be an expanding procession of general tour groups from the Americas and Western Europe. A new age for China travel had begun.

This is not to say that travelers may now blithely pack a bag and board a plane for Peking, much as they might for Rome, Bombay, or Tokyo. Although China appears to be minding less and less *who* comes to visit, *how* and *when* they come are matters that remain subject to a variety of conditions.

The overriding condition—and the one that sets a China visit apart from travel to most other places—is that visitors come to China as part of an organized tour. In 1978, for the first time on any large scale, the specific authority to form such tours was granted to a number of airlines, travel agents, and private organizations. While in China, these tours are conducted according to fixed itineraries arranged by the official China International Travel Service.

Despite the requirements for advanced booking and the rigors of exacting, prearranged scheduling, the initial response to these tour offerings has been overwhelming. And the reaction of the first returned travelers has been almost universally enthusiastic. Whatever the group experience loses in the way of spontaneity, it gains in efficiency. One's time in China is precious. When one begins to consider all that has happened in China and all that is going on there now, barely a moment is to be wasted.

The purpose of this *Guide* is to aid visitors to make the fullest use of their time in China. Although getting there is no longer as arduous a procedure as it was just a few years ago, a number of special steps are still required, especially for special-interest groups or individuals seeking to initiate visits for purposes other than general travel. The first section of the *Guide* includes information on venues and agencies (inside and outside China) for categories of visitors other than general tourists (e.g., professional organizations and business persons). In addition, the *Guide* discusses the special procedures and protocol required by the circumstance of group travel in China.

The section on China itineraries focuses on all major cities and sites included on general tours in the late 1970s. Each city is discussed in a dual context—its importance in traditional China and its significance in the contemporary life of the People's Republic. For the Chinese, the past is used as a means to better serve the present. The pre-eminent stress for visitors is on how China lives today. For that reason, each discussion attempts to account for each city's significance in contemporary China, its role in the revolution, its economy and culture, and its measured achievements in improving life for its citizens. Similarly, under the Highlights section for each city, modern structures, factories, and social institutions are discussed along with monuments from traditional China.

Time for free activity is short. For larger cities, the *Guide* suggests some brief walking tours (usually requiring no more than an hour) to enable maximum use of the free time available. In addition, step-by-step tours of major shopping areas are provided to facilitate "free-lance" excursions.

The last section of the *Guide* contains some useful Chinese phrases, suggestions for background reading, and a special section on the Kwangchow (Canton) Trade Fair.

With a few minor exceptions, the transliteration of Chinese place-names and references follows the Wade-Giles system, the method still most commonly used in the West. For cities, alternate spellings in *Hanyu pinyin* (the PRC's official system) are indicated at the start of each section.

Every effort has been made to present information that is accurate and up-to-date. The authors welcome the comments and criticisms of readers, as well as suggestions for additions to future editions.

ACKNOWLEDGMENTS

The authors wish to express their thanks to the American Region staff of Japan Air Lines for their encouragement, support, and advice in all stages of preparing this GUIDE. Special thanks are given to Mike Nagai and Norman Bacon for their cooperation and patience. Within JAL's New York District Office, Ken Shiba provided that invaluable first spark and Jackie Cole a continual supporting glow.

The staff of Eurasia Press played an indispensable role in assembling, editing, and producing this book. They include Lorna Harbus (Managing Editor), Laurel Hirsch (Editorial Assistant), and Jospeh Duchac. Many good friends of China lent their good sense and experience to the project, notably Esther Gollobin as well as Shao Tzu-ping and Norval Welch. Kathie Brown, Scott Kelly, and Michael Krieger of U.S. Lithograph Inc. are owed a special note of thanks for lending their care and special skills to the book.

A special acknowledgment is due the many friends in China whose gracious hospitality and patient explanations made possible what we hope will be a small contribution to mutual understanding. Many US colleagues shared their insights as well. The National Committee on US-China Relations, the National Council for US-China Trade, and the US-China Peoples Friendship Association were the true pioneers in areas of US-China travel. Much of the information represented here derives from the experience gained through contact with these organizations.

On a more personal level, one can never adequately acknowledge the support of long-standing friends. Arne de Keijzer singles out M. for carrying it all from the beginning and for all that was; B. for fine choruses of "Tangerine;" L. for giving more than a Bookhouse full of wisdom; M. for making Irish pluck contagious; H. for sharing what can be; and his parents for gifts beyond measure.

New York, New York
May 1, 1978

Access to China

A JOURNEY LIKE NO OTHER

A trip to China is unique among travel experiences. The dominant characteristics of the People's Republic of China—its size, cultural heritage, and political environment—suffice to give an impression of a universe unto itself. Moreover, in the course of the past three decades, China has been experiencing a transformation which, in its scope, intensity, and pervasiveness, has few if any parallels in the contemporary world. Whether or not one agrees with its ideological premises, it is evident that the Chinese Revolution and its effects have taken root everywhere—in China's streets, farms, factories, schools, homes—and even in the hotels, restaurants, and conveyances used by tourists. For the Chinese, the economic and social accomplishments of this new era are matters of consuming interest and the source of unconcealed pride and enthusiasm.

Thus, the attention and interest of the visitor may be drawn less to the physical attractions of China, as formidable as these may be, than to the demeanor of its people, whose zeal for nation-building is as keen and unabashed as may be experienced anywhere. Virtually all aspects of work, culture, and even recreation are perceived in terms of their contribution to moving China forward. More than likely, the tourist will find his own visit being addressed in the same light. As a function of state policy, tourism helps to expand the economy and, not incidentally, win more friends for China. Thus, even tourists with the most modest outlook and expectations are apt to find themselves cast in the role of international emissaries, there to build bridges of understanding between their own country and the new society being forged in China. And since foreign visitors are a relatively new phenomenon in the People's Republic—tourism from the West was virtually unheard of in the 1950s and 1960s—they are visible symbols of a new policy that seeks to bridge the vast gulf which has separated China from the West.

Ironically, perhaps, it may be the circumstance of its isolation from the West that has made China an exceptional object of interest. For most visitors, China's past and present have a common remoteness, and while this cultural distance may stimulate a desire to see China, it may also inhibit full appreciation of the experience. There are real cultural distances, and many who put off learning anything about China until their arrival in Peking are likely to leave having absorbed very little.

2

Aside from the special qualities of the country itself, the uniqueness of a trip to China is underscored by how the Chinese organize such travel. The Chinese assume that travelers who have taken the effort to come there have a serious intent to learn about the country and most activities planned for visitors proceed from that assumption. Since a visit to China is seen primarily as a learning experience, the Chinese seek to exert as much control as possible over the content and quality of that experience. Thus, although the treatment of visitors is invariably thoughtful and courteous, the Chinese are not content with a role as affable, fawning hosts. In the short time available (usually less than three weeks), they attempt to convey as coherent and as comprehensive a picture as possible of the salient aspects of their country's social, economic, and cultural development.

It is from this rationale that the highly organized nature of most trips proceeds. Almost all Western visitors (apart from specially invited individuals and those on business ventures) travel as part of an escorted group. Participants sightsee and take most meals together and stay at the same hotels. They are invariably accompanied on their daily excursions by an official interpreter. Tour itineraries are for the most part settled in advance and finalized within a day after arrival in China. Likewise, daily schedules of activities and visits are prearranged around tight (and frequently rigorous) schedules. The time allotted for independent activities is limited, whereas much time is devoted to organized group discussions of what's being seen. Throughout, the visitor's willingness to abide with the special circumstances of China travel is key to maximum use and enjoyment of the experience.

INTRODUCING CHINA

The Chinese People

The People's Republic of China (PRC) is far-and-away the most populous nation on earth. In 1978, the Chinese population totaled over 900 million, making China the home of one out of every five persons in the world. China is also distinguished by one of the oldest continuous civilizations on earth, with roots traced as far back as 2200 BC. The Chinese written language—using a unique, nonalphabetic script—is a thread that links modern-day China with its ancient past. The written script remains constant throughout the land. In its spoken form, however, Chinese has numerous dialects, although about two-thirds of the people can now understand *putunghua*—the national dialect.

The Political System

A revolutionary movement that began in the 1920s culminated in the foundation, on October 1, 1949, of the People's Republic of China. Rejecting both the traditions of China's imperial past and the weak, inept systems that dominated Chinese governments in the first half of the 20th century, the new revolutionary government, under Mao Tse-tung, set out to restructure the country along orthodox Socialist lines.

The highest organ of legislative power in China is the National People's Congress, which elected 3,444 deputies to its fifth session in February 1978. The leading political force in the country, as stipulated by the Constitution, is the Chinese Communist Party. Virtually all major decisions in China—political, economic, and social—are made by the Party and its leadership. Mao Tse-tung, Chairman of the Party from 1949 until his death in 1976, was by virtue of that position the preeminent leader of China. Mao was succeeded as Party chairman in October 1976 by Hua Kuo-feng.

Mao's death in mid-1976 was followed by considerable political turmoil in China. A group of ultraradicals, branded as the "gang of four" and including Chiang Ch'ing, Mao's widow, attempted to usurp state power. By late 1977, however, stability was restored under the leadership of Hua and Teng Hsiao-p'ing, a former target of the gang. The post-Mao period has since been marked by new outpourings in the areas of cultural and political expression, as well as by a renewed emphasis on productivity and new Chinese initiatives towards economic, technological, and cultural exchanges with the West.

The Economic System

China has always been, and remains today, a predominantly agricultural country. For almost three decades prior to 1949, the incessant ravages of civil disorder, foreign interference and aggression, and gross economic neglect had reduced China to a state of helpless dependence. The first task of the new government, therefore, was to restore the economy to levels of self-sufficiency. By the early 1950s, mass starvation had been virtually eliminated and, by the end of the decade, China had begun to mobilize its vast natural and human resources to lay the base for major industrialization. Despite severe setbacks—especially in the early and mid-1960s—China has continued its remarkable expansion, aided by the discovery of tremendous oil reserves and the effective mobilization of the nation's mammoth workforce. Still, China in the mid-1970s remained, by its own admission, an underdeveloped country with large gaps in infrastructure and technology as yet awaiting remedy.

China's economy is centrally planned and centrally controlled, although a considerable degree of local initiative is encouraged in most sectors. A dominant theme in domestic development—as well as in China's trade relations—is self-sufficiency. In the 1970s, foreign trade policies took a dramatic turn as the country sought to broaden its technological and industrial base through major purchases from the West. In an interview in late 1977, a leading Chinese trade official reiterated China's willingness to "develop and expand foreign trade relations with any country on the basis of mutual demand and mutual benefit."

CHINA TRAVEL IN THE 1970s

For more than two decades after its founding, the PRC remained virtually off limits to most travelers from the West. Since 1971, however, restrictions on travel to China by Westerners have been progressively eased. In 1976, approximately 20,000 visitors from Japan, 3,000 from Australia, 3,000 from the US, and 1,200 from the UK visited China. A growing proportion of visitors were business people attending the Canton (Kwangchow) Trade Fair (the fall 1977 fair attracted 30,000 foreign visitors, including 17,000 directly engaged in trading). Some, by virtue of ongoing trade relationships, have become regular visitors to the PRC.

In late 1977 there were indications that PRC policy towards foreign travel was about to take a dramatic new turn. Authorities indicated they would soon seek to vastly increase China's tourist volume. For 1978, some 12,000 trips were approved for the US alone, more than twice the total of 1977. For 1980, the projected total from all countries (excepting Hong Kong) was put at 100,000.

Until 1978, private travel to China had been limited mainly to those who had received a direct invitation from the Chinese government or to groups formed by PRC-oriented organizations officially designated to sponsor such trips. Beginning in 1978, however, China had clearly begun to view foreign travel in a new light. Foreign airlines (including PanAm, Japan Air Lines, Canadian Pacific, and Iranair) and a few commercial travel agents were granted the right to form their own tours to China. Although organized group travel remains the norm, the criteria for selection of travelers in the general tour category has been left largely to the discretion of commercial tour operators. For these groups, virtually all prior requirements for screening of applicants have been set aside, with the result that selections are now made purely on a "first come, first served" basis. The only real limitation on such trips remained the availability of accommodations in China. But here, too, new policies in effect in 1978 aimed at rapid expansion and upgrading of hotel and transportation amenities. Indeed, the era of China's isolation from the myriad of travelers who had waited decades for a chance to visit was apparently drawing to a close.

Categories of China Travelers

Official Visitors. Apart from diplomatic exchanges, the PRC government has tendered official invitations to a variety of individuals and groups to visit China. For the most part, such invitations are issued on the PRC's initiative and usually have some bearing on PRC foreign policy, trade, or national political objectives. Such visits are characterized by sanction from the visitor's government, special status as guests of the host country, and high-level coordination with counterpart organizations in China (e.g., Chinese Academy of Sciences, All-China Sports Federation, China Council for the Promotion of International Trade).

Professional Groups. The Chinese regard these as "people-to-people" exchanges. Groups are composed of 12-20 persons working in a common profession or belonging to a specific professional, civic, or other association. Thus, they are also characterized as "affinity groups." The range of people invited has been broad, from academics (university trustees, high school students) to civic organizations (League of Women Voters, Women for International Understanding), from economists (American Economic Association) to scientists (American Federation of Scientists); from museum curators to dairy farmers.

A common denominator is the professional bond within a group, and the joint submission of a tour proposal to Chinese authorities (such proposals are discussed in the section on "The Application Process").

China-Friendship Delegations. By far the largest number of visitors from the West fall in the category of what the Chinese call "friendship" delegations, the majority of which are formed by private "China-friendship" organizations. Such organizations exist throughout the Western Hemisphere (including more than 100 local chapters in the US and 8 in Canada) as well as in virtually all countries in Western Europe (see listing, pp. 8-9). Their stated purpose is to promote "people-to-people" friendship between China and their own countries. In addition to sponsoring tours, most engage in volunteer educational and cultural activities that promote general-level interest in China. These are not "political" organizations *per se*, and most eschew involvement in issues not directly tied to China. With respect to China's revolutionary practices and goals, many see themselves as interpreters (rather than advocates) of Chinese policy. All maintain liaison with the Chinese People's Association for Friendship with Foreign Countries in Peking.

Friendship tour participants are drawn from a variety of occupations and interest groups, including students, professionals, farmers, and factory workers, as well as representatives of minority groups, community agencies, trade unions, and political organizations. For such tours, an informal national quota system has apparently been in force, with Japan and the US allotted large contingents into the late 1970s. Many tours are set aside for members of China-friendship organizations (such membership is open to all who seek to join). Groups pay their own way (scholarships may be available for low-income members) and usually are allotted 16-21 day itineraries. Their visits are arranged through the China International Travel Service. These tours usually seek to focus on specific aspects of China's economic, social, and political development, although cultural sites are also part of their itineraries.

China Friendship Associations in Australia, Japan, North and South America, and Western Europe

Australia
Australia-China Society. 228 Gertrude Street, Fitzroy 3065, Victoria

Canada
Canada-China Friendship Association. Box 3304, Halifax, Nova Scotia

Canada-China Friendship Association. CP 872, Station A, Montreal, Quebec

Canada-China Friendship Association. 3630 Argyle St., *or* Box 3531 Regina, Saskatchewan

Canada-Friendship Association. Box 373, Station Q, Toronto, Ontario

Canada-China Friendship Association. 33 East Hastings, Vancouver, 4, British Columbia

Canada-China Friendship Association. Box 5074, Station B, Victoria, British Columbia

Canada-China Friendship Association. 2862 Henderson Hwy., Winnipeg, Manitoba

Canada-China Friendship Association. Box 305, Wolfville, Nova Scotia

Colombia
Asociación dela Amistad Colombo-China. A.A. 17028, Bogata

Denmark
Venskabsforbundet Danmark-Kina. Studiesstraede 18, DK 1455 Copenhagen

Venskabsforbundet Danmark-Kina. Ravnsborg Tvaergade, 2200 Copenhagen N

Federal Republic of Germany
Gesellschaft für Deutsch-Chinesische Freundschaft. Dreysestrasse 17, 1000 Berlin 21

Gesellschaft für Deutsch-Chinesische Freundschaft. Postbach 16328, 6000 Frankfurt Am Main

Italy
Associazione Italia-Cina. Via del Seminario 87, Roma

Japan
Japan-China Friendship Association. 1-4 Nishiki-cho, Kanda, Chivodaka, Tokyo

Mexico
Sociedad Amigos de China Popular, A.C. Peten 460 Col. Vertiz Navarte, Mexico 12, D.F.

Netherlands
Netherlands-China Friendship Association. Bermuurde,-Weerd OZ 8, Utrecht

Norway
Vennskapsambandit Norge-Kina. Boks 57, Blindern, Oslo

Sweden
Svenski-Kinesiska Vanskapsfobundet. Maria Prastgardsgata 31, Stockholm, 11652
Svenski-Kinesiska Vanskapsfobundet. Malmoavdelningen Box 4180, Malmo

UK
Society for Anglo-Chinese Understanding. 152 Camden High Street, London, NW 1, England

General Tour Groups. Until 1977, the Chinese discouraged tourism *per se* (except for overseas Chinese), both for political reasons and due to a lack of adequate facilities and sufficient numbers of qualified escorts and interpreters. The first tourists to break this pattern were cruise ship passengers who were allowed entry to one or two cities on the basis of a "shore pass" of two to three days. By late 1977, most international airlines having a relationship with the Civil Aviation Administration of China (CAAC—China's national airline) were also allocated tour groups and, as of early 1978, two travel agents in the US were each granted tours totaling 150-200 people. The largest beneficiary of the new policy has been the China-friendship organizations. The US-China Peoples Friendship Association had in the past been granted the right to form 26 "friendship" tours per year (of 24 persons each). In 1978, it was given an allocation of some 2,600 trips, including 22 general "study" tours of 12-day duration. As with the tours formed by airlines, these groups need not be organized around a particular professional focus, require no prior organizational ties, and are generally filled on a "first come, first served" basis.

The general tours also adhere to a new format. The size of the groups has been expanded to 100 and is broken down into smaller "clusters" once inside China. They generally follow a standard itinerary (Peking, Shanghai, Hangchow, Kwangchow (Canton)—although Japan Air Lines offers a more varied itinerary. All are hosted by China International Travel Service.

Prospective visitors in this category are advised to be cautious in dealing with travel agencies advertising tours to China. There have been unfortunate incidents involving payments of nonrefundable deposits for tours never authorized. Persons or companies offering tours to China should be double-checked through airlines, shipping companies, or the official and private organizations listed in this *Guide*.

Business Travelers. Of the 4,000 North and South Americans who visited China in 1977, more than half came for business purposes. Most of these were invited to attend the semi-annual Chinese Export Commodities Fair held in Kwangchow (see special section on the Fair, p. 193), although others have also visited Peking and Shanghai. Business people are invited only on the basis of carrying out trade; they rarely have the opportunity to see much of China beyond the negotiating sites. On the other hand, technicians working on plant construction in more remote parts of China get a glimpse of daily Chinese life withheld from most other visitors.

Invitations to representatives of business enterprises are arranged through one of China's nine state-owned trade corporations (listed on p.196). The Chinese have also invited commercial groups such as chambers of commerce, the Mid-America Committee, and the National Machine Tool Builders Association.

Travel from the United States

Exchanges on a significant scale between the US and the PRC began in March 1971 when the US travel ban to China was formally lifted. The Shanghai Communiqué, issued in 1972, noted that exchange visits were an essential part of the process of normalizing relations between the two countries. From 1972 until early 1978, a total of about 15,000 persons from the US had visited China, with visa applications for that same period estimated at 200,000. In turn, about 1,000

Chinese have visited the US, for the most part trade and scientific specialists. During March-April 1978, in a notable exchange, leading officials of the China International Travel Service toured the US, visiting tourist sites and meeting with various representatives of the US travel industry.

Official Contacts. Official US exchanges with the People's Republic of China began in 1971 when Premier Chou En-lai personally invited the US Table Tennis Team to China. Secretary of State Kissinger soon followed. President Nixon's famous visit in February 1972 resulted in the issuance of the Shanghai Communiqúe, a document that expressed a desire on the part of both governments to work towards normal relations. Although by 1978 normalization had not been achieved, cultural, scientific, and commercial exchanges have taken place by arrangement of both governments. President Ford and officials of the Carter administration have since visited China, as have 70 US senators and congressmen.

Quasi-Official Contacts. Three nongovernmental organizations, the National Committee on US-China Relations, the National Council for US-China Trade, and the Committee on Scholarly Communication with the People's Republic of China, handle what might be considered quasi-official exchanges in trade, science, technology, medicine, culture, and sports. Such exchanges and visits have been agreed to in principle by the two governments and are nominally hosted by them. Logistics and administration, however, are handled by the staff of the three organizations.

Within their areas of specialty, the three groups can advise on the likely success of a travel request, provide names of appropriate contacts in China, offer reports on previous visits in specific fields, and supply general background information. Delegations specifically organized by them, however, consist largely of officials or influential public figures, and are not accessible to the general public.

The National Committee on US-China Relations, Inc. (NCUSCR). 777 United Nations Plaza, 9b, New York, New York 10017.

The NCUSCR facilitates and administers exchange visits agreed to by the US and PRC governments in the fields of education, international affairs, performing arts, and sports. In the absence of full diplomatic relations between the US and China, the NCUSCR administers activities normally managed through direct government channels. It is funded largely by the US Department of State, and works under its direction. Some of its major undertakings have included visits to China by the Philadelphia Orchestra (1973), a group of university presidents (1974), a track and field team (1975), and a group of congressional committee staff members. Groups from China have included a martial arts troupe (1974), a women's basketball team (1975), and a delegation from the Chinese People's Institute for Foreign Affairs (1977). General services of the National Committee include travel advice, briefing kits, seminars, and a newsletter describing its programs. Also available are lists of previous exchange groups who may be contacted for more specific information.

Committee on Scholarly Communication with the People's Republic of China (CSCPRC). National Academy of Sciences, 2101 Constitution Avenue, N.W., Washington, D.C. 20418.

The CSCPRC is sponsored jointly by the National Academy of Sciences, the American Council of Learned Societies, and the Social Science Research Council. It is supported in part by State Department funding and administers exchanges in science, medicine, and technology. Sponsored groups are selected on the basis of prior negotiation with the PRC government. The CSCPRC hopes to inaugurate a student exchange program following the establishment of formal diplomatic relations.

The National Council for US-China Trade (NCUSCT). 1050 17th Street, N.W., Washington, D.C. 20036.

The NCUSCT is recognized by both governments as the focal point for development of trade between China and the US. This organization is less directly connected to the US government than either the NCUSCR or the CSCPRC, as it derives its financial support from some 390 member corporations, banks, and individuals, and because the Chinese have been willing to move outside of government channels to engage in foreign trade and commerce. The NCUSCT assists both members and nonmembers in formulating approaches to Chinese foreign trade authorities. It assists business persons in making appropriate contacts, sponsors commercial exchanges between the two countries, and offers special services to persons attending the Kwangchow Trade Fair.

It also maintains special industry-wide committees to help promote US-China trade. The NCUSCT publishes a bimonthly magazine for members entitled *China Business Review*, with special reports on different sectors of the Chinese economy, and maintains a translation service to aid in rendering business proposals into Chinese.

Private Exchanges. The largest number of US citizens to visit China prior to 1978 traveled under the auspices of the US-China Peoples Friendship Association (USCPFA). Other organizationally based or *ad hoc* groups in the US have succeeded in arranging tours through direct application to China International Travel Service (CITS) in Peking. In 1977-78, such tours included artists, World War II veterans, religious leaders, and overseas Chinese. In 1978, CITS also granted trips to trade union leaders, media specialists, women financial executives, and booksellers.

US-China Peoples Friendship Association (USCPFA). National Office: 635 South Westlake Avenue, Los Angeles, California 90057.

The USCPFA is recognized by the Chinese as the principal sponsor of "friendship" tours to the PRC for US citizens. A non-profit educational organization founded in 1974, the USCPFA's status and purpose is similar to those of friendship organizations in other countries that are actively sympathetic to China. It supports the establishment of full diplomatic relations with China, the severance of all official US ties with Taiwan, and the development of "people-to-people" contacts between the US and China. USCPFA tours (about 100 per year) are organized regionally (by its 110 member chapters) as well as around special interests such as community organizations, trade unions, sports, minority leaders, public-health personnel, and curriculum planners. In 1978, the USCPFA sponsored 2,600 visits to the PRC (compared with 675 in 1977), with 5,000 scheduled for 1979. The first reciprocal "people-to-people" exchange from China took place in December 1977, with the visit to the US of an artist delegation sponsored by the Chinese People's Association for Friendship with Foreign Countries. USCPFA tours are organized according to a variety of formats and are available to non-members as well as members. In 1978, the cost of USCPFA general tours to China was $2,600 (including airfare and 12 days in the PRC).

Travel From Canada

Canada established diplomatic relations with the PRC in 1969. Since then, successive governmental exchange agreements have been concluded annually. Canada sends only government personnel from various ministries on these missions. The government also monitors the student exchange program between the two countries. The Council for the Arts administers officially sponsored tours of Chinese cultural groups. In March 1978, in an event of major cultural significance, the Toronto Symphony Orchestra engaged in a major tour of Chinese cities. Additional exchanges are carried out through private channels, most of which are handled through the eight branches of the Canada-China Friendship Association. In 1978, Canadian Pacific

Airlines was awarded the right to organize China tours for 1,000 visitors.

Travel from Japan

Japan's broad and multichanneled relationship with China is reflected in the wide diversity of contacts between Tokyo and Peking. The two governments regularly exchange delegations, but the Chinese also unilaterally invite opposition political parties, political leaders, and special-interest groups. Japan also has a number of friendship groups that sponsor private visits. Prominent among these is the Japan-China Friendship Association (Orthodox).

Sports exchanges are popular between the two countries. They are sponsored by the appropriate national organizations as well as by universities, commercial enterprises, and military groups. Cultural exchanges are administered under a government umbrella organization but are usually initiated by private interests.

Travel from the United Kingdom

The United Kingdom was one of the first Western countries to recognize the PRC after its founding in 1949, and the British have had a good working relationship with China since then. A great many British groups have visited the PRC, among them labor groups, friendship delegations, sports teams, and technical delegations. The UK has an official trade promotion organization called the Sino-British Trade Council, but the Chinese also deal with a private consortium known as the "48 Group," comprising a number of firms that were the first to publicly promote trade with China. Exchange agreements are reviewed annually by the two governments. A number of private tours are arranged each year through the Society for Anglo-Chinese Understanding (SACU), the UK's China-friendship organization.

THE APPLICATION PROCESS

Despite the increased tourist volume planned for the late 1970s, procedures for gaining entry to China were expected to remain relatively formal and lengthy, calling for long-range planning and awareness of special guidelines. And, although in 1978 the PRC was moving closer to acceptance of general tourism, it seemed likely that a degree of selectivity would be retained, at least for those seeking to pursue specific interests while in China. For example, special restrictions may continue to apply to Western journalists (including photo-journalists) and to citizens of countries that do not have full diplomatic ties with the PRC, as well as to persons with political associations considered inimical to state interests (i.e., persons with ongoing political or commercial ties to the present government on Taiwan).

Inasmuch as the number of applicants is expected to continue to outpace the availability of accommodations in China, preference (apart from participants in general tours formed by airlines and travel agents) will no doubt continue to be given to applicants whose interests or occupations have a clear counterpart in China and, by extension, to those whose experience in China is likely to have a broad impact on the occupational or social circles to which they return. Although such criteria have remained vague and largely unspecified, the Chinese seem likely to continue to regard an invitation to visit to their country as a privilege to be conferred on those either well-placed or well-disposed to "spread the good word" to their associates back home.

Special-Interest Travel

Groups seeking to initiate a visit to China in order to pursue a special interest (i.e., commercial or professional) must be in possession of an official invitation from a PRC governmental body. The key element in securing an invitation is a written proposal. Except in the case of persons well known in China, individual applicants will usually be advised to seek entry as part of a group.

In general, a short good-will tour is the easiest to arrange. A wide variety of occupational groups has succeeded in gaining approval, with medical, educational, legal, and technical fields accounting for a significant share. In recent years, the Chinese have been known to turn down the following proposals: a hike along the length of the Great Wall, a canoe trip down the Yangtse River, a bicycle tour of southern provinces, a mobile home trip by a retired couple, a mountain-climbing team, in-depth studies at institutes or universities, schemes for "living among the people," projects of "humanitarian" interests (e.g., missionary groups).

Once a prospective group has been formed, a detailed letter requesting permission to visit China should be prepared and addressed to the China International Travel Service or to an appropriate PRC host organization. The letter should include the following elements:

Reason for the Visit. Applicants should explain why, from the group's vantage point, they seek to make the trip; why the Chinese should invite this particular group; the manner in which the trip will contribute to mutual understanding, friendship, and professional knowledge.

Short Biographies of Participants. Chinese travel authorities seek a clear sense of the composition and balance of a group and the relevance of each member to it. For example, for special-interest groups, married couples should not seek to travel on the same trip unless both spouses have demonstrable ties to the group's interest.

Length and Time of Year for the Proposed Trip. Most group visits last from two to three weeks. In terms of comfort, the best times for visiting China are in spring and fall.

Proposed Activities While in China. Although a list of activities need not be exhaustive, proposals should include the kinds of institutions deemed relevant to the group's interests (universities, museums, factories, historical sites). The more specific the list, the better, although the final itinerary will consist mainly of what's practicable from the Chinese end.

Places to Be Visited. Most groups, as a matter of course, travel to Peking, Shanghai, and Kwangchow. Other cities commonly visited include Sian, Nanking, Shenyang, and Hangchow. Requests to visit specific cities or regions should be rationalized in terms of the group's special focus. Proposals may also include general suggestions for visiting a rural commune, although the specific selection is best left to the Chinese. Rural sojourns are usually kept short, so as not to overtax local facilities or unduly disrupt work schedules.

Official Travel Contacts in the PRC

Final authority for granting permission to visit China is vested in a small number of central agencies in Peking. Initial applications from all organizations, groups, and individuals must receive approval (usually transmitted in the form of an invitation to visit China) from

Chairman Mao Tse-tung Memorial Hall, Peking

one of these agencies. In general, initial travel requests may also be sent to the PRC's overseas diplomatic representatives. Although the embassies are not themselves empowered to extend invitations, they may expedite such requests and handle visas and other formalities.

China International Travel Service. The China International Travel Service (CITS) carries out two functions: On the international level, it has responsibility for all general tour groups, i.e., those that come for nonprofessional reasons. On the domestic level, it makes all arrangements for travel within the People's Republic of China. Most tour groups should apply to this organization; they will probably be referred to it should they apply through a Chinese diplomatic mission abroad. The CITS address is 6 East Changan, Peking.

While not maintaining any offices overseas, CITS has an official agent in Hong Kong: the China Travel Service (CTS), whose main office is at 77 Queens Road, Central, Hong Kong. Until 1978, CTS was only authorized to assist groups or individuals already in possession of an invitation from a host organization in China. Currently, however, it is empowered to approve individual visits (by business persons or overseas Chinese) and form group tours on its own. In fact, by February 1978, CTS was granting many visas on as little as 24-hours' notice.

Although CITS has no other agents acting on its behalf in other countries, it does maintain correspondence with a number of private travel agencies in Japan, Canada, the US, Latin America, and Europe, and, through them, grants allocations for general and specialized groups.

PRC Agencies for Specialized Travel

A variety of organizations in China issue invitations to foreign delegations, although most of these exchanges are arranged through government (or quasi-official) channels at the other end and rarely come about as the result of private initiatives. Although it is possible for private groups to contact these agencies directly (all are headquartered in Peking), the likelihood of a positive response—except in the case of overseas Chinese—is not great.

Overseas Chinese Travel Service. This organization handles all travel requests and arrangements for overseas Chinese, whether born in China or not. Visitors of Chinese origin are generally accorded trips of longer duration. While in China, they may travel in smaller groups or singly.

Chinese People's Institute of Foreign Affairs. An advisory and research body, the institute usually invites prominent public figures and government officials. Opinion leaders, members of the political opposition, influential journalists, or prominent business figures are handled under the auspices of this institute.

Chinese People's Association for Friendship with Foreign Countries. This association invites cultural figures, orchestras, artists, dance companies, and other groups concerned with art, literature, and other cultural interests. It maintains a consultative relationship with overseas China-friendship associations in non-Communist countries.

All-China Sports Federation. This federation invites foreign athletic teams and sponsors international competitions in China.

Chinese Scientific and Technical Association. This group is almost a direct counterpart of the US Committee on Scholarly Communication with the People's Republic of China. It seeks to bring scientists and scholars to China.

China Medical Assocation. This agency invites medical delegations.

China Council for the Promotion of International Trade. This group's counterpart in the US is the National Council for US-China Trade. It arranges exchanges of business and commercial delegations.

Chinese Architecture Society. To date, a group of US women architects, among others, has been invited to China by the society.

Chinese Ministry of Education. This agency invites educational administrators as well as delegations from foreign schools and universities.

China's State Trading Corporations

Foreign trade in the PRC is a state monopoly, controlled by the Ministry of Foreign Trade and conducted through nine foreign trade corporations. The corporations are organized according to kinds of commodities, and businesses seeking to initiate trade—either import or export—can do so by writing directly to the appropriate foreign trade corporation (see listing, p. 196).

The most important event on the China trade calendar is the semi-annual Chinese Export Commodities Fair, held in Kwangchow (Canton) during April 15-May 15 and October 15-November 15. Invitations to the Fair may be solicited by contacting the appropriate foreign trade corporation.

Hong Kong's China Resources Company, an official agency of the PRC, is authorized to deal directly with foreign business persons. This company handles commercial matters for the Chinese corporations dealing with machinery, chemicals, and metals and minerals. It also acts as an intermediary for the China National Technical Import Corporation.

PRC Diplomatic Missions Abroad

In general, PRC diplomatic missions deal with governmental exchanges rather than with private travel requests, although special sections may be available to assist commercial travelers and overseas Chinese. Since permission to visit China can be secured only from an appropriate host organization in Peking (and not from a PRC embassy), inquiries regarding general travel—especially in the case of first trips—are likely to be redirected to CITS.

Diplomatic representatives may occasionally grant appointments to professional groups wishing to visit China. They may be helpful in framing a proposal, indicating the appropriate agency to write to in Peking and informally evaluating the merits of the application. Commercial sections of embassies or liaison offices are more active in arranging travel. In addition to contacting the appropriate foreign trade corporation in Peking, traders are advised to seek assistance from these sections.

The Liaison Office of the PRC in the US. The Liaison Office of the People's Republic of China to the United States plays an important role in evaluating travel and trade proposals. Once an invitation

Selected Overseas Diplomatic Missions of the PRC

Argentina. Conesa 1964, Buenos Aires, Argentina

Australia. 247 Federal Highway, Watson, Canberra, 2600 Australia

Belgium. Boulevard General Jacques, #19, 1050 Brussels

Brazil. Embaixad Republica Popular da China, MPWS cj 43 It 4, Brazilia, DF, Brazil

Canada. 411-415 St. Andrews St., Ottawa, Ontario K1N 5H3

Colombia. Carrera 15 80-25, Bogota

Denmark. Oregaardsalle #25, DK 2900 Hellerup, Copenhagen

France. 11 Avenue George V, 75008, Paris

FRG. 5307 Wachtbergniederbachen, Konrad-Adenauer Str. 104

Italy. Via Giovanne, Paiseillo 39, Roma 00198

Japan. 5-30 Minami-Azabu, 4-Chome, Minato-ku, Tokyo

Mexico. Avenue San Geronimo 217, Mexico City 20, DF

Netherlands. Adriaan Goehooplaan 7, Den Haag 070-55.15.15

Norway. 11 Inkognitojaten, Oslo 12

Peru. Jr. Jose Granda 150, San Isidoro, Lima

Sweden. Bragevagen #4, Stockholm

United Kingdom. 31 Portland Place, London W1N 3AG

United States. (Liaison Office), 2300 Connecticut Avenue, N.W., Washington, D.C. 20008

Venezuela. Quinta Mama, Calle Mohedne, Country Club, Caracas

---

has been received from the host organization in China, the Washington office will also process visas. A copy of trade or travel proposals sent to China should be forwarded to the Liaison Office, with a covering request to discuss the proposal further. The Commercial Section of the Liaison Office can provide assistance in making introductions in China, in ascertaining whether there is interest in the kind of business proposed, and in solving problems once a commercial relationship has been established.

INTERNATIONAL TRAVEL CONNECTIONS

While China may still seem "on the other side of the world"—psychologically and culturally—getting there is no longer an exotic or complicated procedure.

Air Links. The most common points of entry into China by air are Peking and Shanghai. The major rail connection is from Hong Kong to Kwangchow (Canton). In all cases, the entry and exit points will be specified by China International Travel Service. All travel connections within China are prearranged.

Ten international carriers now fly directly to Peking or Shanghai. For those living in North and South America, the Pacific is the shortest route, with direct flights via Tokyo available on Japan Air Lines and several other carriers (see chart below). Connections via the Atlantic and Europe are also possible. For those living on the Atlantic seaboard this route may mean a modest financial saving. Atlantic routings entail a longer flight time, however, since there are at least three stops en route to China, often including a change of planes and, usually, an overnight layover in Switzerland, Romania, or Pakistan.

DIRECT FLIGHTS TO
THE PEOPLE'S REPUBLIC OF CHINA

Via Europe, Africa, and Western Asia

Departure Day	Originating City	Airline	Destination
Monday	Athens	Swissair	Peking
	Karachi	Tarom	Peking
Tuesday	Teheran	Iranair	Peking
Wednesday	Addis Ababa	Ethiopian	Peking
	Bombay	Ethiopian	Peking
Wednesday	Karachi	CAAC	Peking
	Paris	CAAC	Peking

Departure Day	Originating City	Airline	Destination
Thursday	Karachi	PIA	Peking
	Moscow	CAAC	Peking
Saturday	Athens	Air France	Peking
	Bucharest	CAAC	Peking
	Moscow	Aeroflot	Peking
	Paris	Air France	Peking
	Teheran	Iraniar	Peking
	Tirana	CAAC	Peking
Sunday	Addis Ababa	Ethiopian	Peking
	Athens	Swissair	Peking
	Bombay	Ethiopian	Peking
	Bucharest	Tarom	Peking
	Geneva	Swissair	Peking
	Karachi	Air France	Peking
		PIA	Peking
	Rawalpindi	PIA	Peking
	Teheran	PIA	Peking
	Zurich	Swissair	Peking

Via Eastern Asia

Departure Day	Originating City	Airline	Destination
Monday	Osaka	JAL	Peking
		JAL	Shanghai
	Tokyo	Air France	Peking
		JAL	Peking
		PIA	Peking
		JAL	Shanghai
Tuesday	Tokyo	CAAC	Peking
Wednesday	Tokyo	Iranair	Peking
		JAL	Peking
Friday	Osaka	CAAC	Peking
		CAAC	Shanghai
	Tokyo	PIA	Peking
		CAAC	Shanghai
Saturday	Pyongyang	CAAC	Peking
Sunday	Tokyo	Iranair	Peking

Note: Schedules as of January 1978.

Arriving by air in Peking or Shanghai, passengers first proceed to customs for a passport check. A representative from the group's host organization will then assist the delegation in moving through customs (waived for official groups who are guests of the state). From Shanghai Airport, most hotels can be reached in about 15 minutes by bus or taxi; in Peking, the trip takes about 40 minutes.

The Hong Kong-Kwangchow Rail Link. Kwangchow is a popular gateway for business people attending the China Export Commodities Fair. The appropriate procedure for groups as well as for individual business travelers is to contact China Travel Service (CTS) in Hong Kong upon arrival. CTS acts as agent for the China International Travel Service in Peking; it issues the railway tickets for the journey from Hong Kong to Kwangchow and arranges all necessary transfers. CTS charges a hefty service charge—although the actual cost of the round-trip ticket is about US$10.00, CTS charges $45.00 for its "service coupon."

If the traveler arrives in Hong Kong by mid-day, arrangements can usually be made to enter China the following morning (assuming a visa has been obtained beforehand). Otherwise, a day's layover in Hong Kong is required. This time is not necessarily wasted, however, since some respite may be needed to overcome "jet-lag."

CTS will inform the visitor of the time of departure from the new railway station in Kowloon. The 1-hour, 15-minute ride to the border passes small plots of land, fishing villages with boats riding at their moorings, several large construction projects, and a couple of market towns. Upon arrival at the border, passengers disembark to pass through British emigration. They then walk across the covered railway bridge into China, where passports are handed to border guards. The next stop is a health station and then on to the Customs House to await baggage inspection. By this time, representatives from the group's host organization (usually CITS) will have made themselves known. They will assist the group through customs and brief it on the procedures and schedule to follow. When these formalities are completed, the visitor can change money and enjoy lunch, which is served at noon (Hong Kong and China are both in the GMT+8 time zone). The train for Kwangchow leaves at 1:00 PM. All seats are preassigned.

As the train pulls out of the station, the contrast with Hong Kong becomes readily apparent: the coaches are well-appointed, air-conditioned, and spotless. The track is smooth, and the peaceful countryside rolls by in a remarkably orderly array. Music is played (sometimes obtrusively) over the loudspeaker, occasionally interrupted by an announcer itemizing the rules and regulations of Chinese train travel (e.g., no spitting). Floors are mopped, mugs of tea are served. A short 1 hour, 50 minutes later the train completes its 90-mile ride to Kwangchow.

Representatives from the group's host organization will be waiting at the railway station. The group will be made to feel immediately welcome and relaxed; it is in the hands of what is widely regarded as the most efficient and pleasant hospitality system in the world. The delegation will be escorted through the modern (and cavernous) Kwangchow Railway Station (the lobby features huge portraits of Mao Tse-tung and Hua Kuo-feng) to waiting transportation.

Business people attending the Fair must go it alone through this process, both at the border and upon arrival at Kwangchow. They should follow the crowds to waiting buses or taxis (the latter have usually been reserved by early arrivals to rush their colleagues off to the hotel). Hotel buses go directly to the Tung Fang (close by) or the Bai Yun (20 minutes away).

Customs Procedures

The most important document the visitor must fill out before arrival is the customs declaration form. It requires an itemization of cameras, watches, jewelry, and money being taken in. Foreigners who are not residents of the PRC are allowed to bring 'in four bottles of liquor, three cartons of cigarettes, an unlimited amount of medicine for personal use, any personal effects, and a virtually unlimited quantity of currency (the amount to be declared).

There is no restriction on film, but professional film equipment (i.e., 16 mm. or 35 mm. cameras) is not allowed in without special permission. There is no restriction on tape recorders and recording tape.

Overseas Chinese or foreign citizens of Chinese origin who come to visit relatives are placed in a special category under Chinese customs laws; these travelers should consult the PRC Liaison Office in Washington or their PRC embassy for further information.

There are four cardinal rules to observe with respect to customs procedures:

1. Declare everything that is asked for.

2. Do not attempt to bring in any contraband or other illegal items (e.g., weapons, drugs).

3. All personal possessions taken into China must be taken out

(cameras, watches, jewelry). In no case should such items be given away. Losses should be reported as soon as they are discovered.

4. Scrupulously record the full amount of money (including travelers checks) taken in. Save all currency-exchange vouchers and all receipts for major purchases. Upon departure, the amount of money taken out must be noted on the original currency declaration form, and should correlate with the amount spent in China. Chinese currency may not be taken out of China (except Bank of China travelers checks).

THE CHINA TRAVELER'S CHECK LIST

What to Pack

For visits to the People's Republic of China, just as to other parts of the world, a simple rule applies: bring twice as much money as may be needed and half as many clothes.

The Chinese are an informal people, therefore obviating the need to pack formal clothing, several changes in wardrobe, or any "special" items for a special occasion. Women will find pantsuits, everyday dresses, and other casual clothing appropriate, and should minimize flamboyance, makeup, and jewelry. Such adornments will seem out of place in China. Shorts, halters, or other revealing clothes are frowned upon.

Men should choose a wardrobe of conservative color. For most visitors there is no need to take anything more formal than a sports jacket and, perhaps, one tie. Shorts are acceptable for men in the summer, as are jeans for both men and women.

Only a few changes of clothing are necessary. Laundry and dry cleaning services are excellent in China, and are usually performed overnight in most hotels. Comfortable walking shoes are a must, perhaps with a dressier pair reserved for dinners or special occasions (women should avoid high heels).

The seasons must be taken into account, of course, and in cool weather it is better to wear several layers than to rely on bulky outer garments. In the winter, warm socks, thermal underwear, and headgear are recommended for both men and women. A sweater is appropriate for almost any time of year, as is a light raincoat. Cottons are most comfortable for hot weather. Open-neck short-sleeved shirts will blend in with the attire of Chinese guides.

Other practical items to include are:

Toiletries. Facial tissues, toothpaste, shampoo. (As most brands can be replenished in Hong Kong, quantities should be kept to a minimum).

Pharmaceuticals. Prescription medicines, vitamins, aspirin, and other health aids as required on a regular basis. As a precaution, cold and digestive remedies might be included. Mosquito repellent can also be useful.

Books. There are no Western publications available in China, so magazines, books, and maps may be brought along.

Liquor and tobacco. Western scotch or liquor is unobtainable in China and the ubiquitous Chinese cigarettes may seem strong and raw to Western tastes.

Camera and film. The rule about film is that one can never take enough. Western film brands are generally unavailable in China (and time considerations usually do not permit developing). An ample supply of batteries, flashbulbs, and, for the fastidious, replacement parts, should also be brought along.

Instant coffee. Many find the Chinese variety quite palatable, but those who are particular should bring their own.

What not to pack. "Street" drugs, pornography, firearms, inflammatory political or evangelical literature, contraband.

WHEN IN CHINA

Climate

Visitors to the PRC should be prepared to experience a wide range of climatic conditions, particularly if visits are made during the spring and autumn when temperature changes can be frequent and abrupt. The enormous north-south extent of Chinese territory—roughly from the latitude of Winnipeg to that of Jamaica—in part explains the great contrasts.

Before discussing specific regions, several general characterizations about China's climate can be made:

—Seasonal temperatures differ greatly in nearly all parts of the country.

—Although rain and high humidity are common in summer throughout the PRC, the length of the rainy season is longer and the amount of rainfall considerably greater south of the Yangtse River.

—Winters are dry with little precipitation, particularly in the north and northeast where spring may also bring little rain.

Northeast. This area includes Shenyang and Harbin, and comprises the huge northeast plain that extends some 600 miles north-south. Summers are hot and dry, and winters bitterly cold; the climate overall is similar to that of Minnesota and southern Alberta.

North-central. This region includes the middle and lower valley of the Yellow River, the intensively cultivated North China Plain, and the hills and mountains to the west. Cities in this area include Peking, Chengchow, and Sian. Temperatures are roughly similar to that of Kansas or Nebraska although there is year-round precipitation. Haze and duststorms can occur during late winter and early spring.

Southeast. The lower Yangtse valley and its many tributaries are characterized by warm temperatures and substantial rainfall. Rice is grown in virtually all lowlands and the long growing season permits at least two crops a year in most regions. Climatic conditions are semitropical, comparable to the Gulf Coast (except that winter storms are rare). Summers are long, hot, and sticky, often subject to incessant rain. The fall is more pleasant, and winters are brief with cooler temperatures. Shanghai and Hangchow are often overcast, damp, and drizzly during the winter.

TEMPERATURE AND PRECIPITATION CHART

Mean Readings*	January (°F)	(°C)	April (°F)	(°C)	July (°F)	(°C)	October (°F)	(°C)
Peking								
Max.	35	1.7	69	20.5	89	31.7	69	20.5
Min.	14	10	43	6.2	71	21.7	44	6.7
Precip.	.2		.7		9.6		.6	
Shanghai								
Max.	47	8.3	67	19.5	91	32.8	75	23.9
Min.	32	0.0	49	9.5	75	23.9	56	13.3
Precip.	1.9		3.6		5.8		2.9	
Kwangchow								
Max.	65	18.3	77	25.0	91	32.8	85	29.5
Min.	49	9.5	65	18.3	77	25.0	67	19.5
Precip.	.9		6.8		8.1		3.4	
Kweilin								
Max.	55	13.1	74	23.4	93	33.9	81	27.2
Min.	41	5.0	59	15.0	76	24.5	62	16.7
Precip.	1.6		9.4		8.0		2.6	
Changsha								
Max.	45	7.2	70	21.1	94	34.5	75	23.9
Min.	35	1.7	56	13.3	78	25.6	59	15.0
Precip.	1.9		5.7		4.4		3.0	
Wuhan								
Max.	46	7.8	69	20.5	93	33.9	74	23.4
Min.	34	1.1	55	12.8	78	25.6	60	15.6
Precip.	1.8		5.8		7.0		3.1	
Chengchow								
Max.	40	4.4	70	21.1	90	32.2	70	21.1
Min.	20	−6.6	50	10.0	70	21.1	50	10.0
Precip.	.4		.9		7.0		.7	
Nanking								
Max.	58	14.5	70	21.1	93	33.4	80	26.7
Min.	24	4.4	45	7.2	75	23.9	60	15.6
Precip.	2.1		4.2		5.0		2.8	
Shenyang								
Max.	20	−6.6	55	12.8	78	25.6	58	14.6
Min.	2	−16.7	40	45	7.2	38	3.3	
Precip.	.2		.8		9.2		1.0	

*Daily readings for temperatures; monthly readings (in inches) for precipitation.

Language

Visitors to the People's Republic of China can expect that tour escorts and representatives from their host organization will speak the group's language, be it English, French, Spanish, or Urdu. These personnel have been trained at universities or special language institutes and are often quite skilled at discoursing with foreigners on many subjects—from politics to culture. Some younger escorts still in training may not be quite so proficient. The flow of conversation will be aided if visitors take care to speak slowly and distinctly, avoid jargon, and adopt a patient demeanor.

English and other foreign languages are now taught over the radio, and one may be greeted on the street with a friendly "Hello!" However, it is not common for most Chinese to speak a foreign language. In all parts of China, the dominant dialect is *putunghua* (the "common language"), a derivative of Peking dialect (sometimes referred to as "Mandarin"). The individual native dialect of each region (e.g., Shanghai, Kwangtung, Hunan) is also used, making most Chinese effectively "bilingual." Of course, any attempt to master some rudimentary Chinese phrases (no matter how horrendous the resulting pronunciation) will be appreciated (see Traveler's Vocabulary, p. 202).

Currency

China's Currency. The official name for the currency of the People's Republic of China is the *renminbi* (RMB—the "people's money"). It is denominated into the *yuan*. Within China, it is also informally counted out as *k'uai* (unit). Yuan notes are printed in denominations of 1, 2, 5, and 10 yuan. The yuan is in turn divided into *fen* (cents). Paper notes are issued for the 50-fen unit (called 5 *jiao*), the 20-fen unit (called 2 *jiao*), and the 10-fen unit (called 1 *jiao*). Coins are in denominations of 1, 2, and 5 fen.

The RMB is not traded on international markets and can be purchased or exchanged only within China or in Hong Kong (in exchange for travelers checks only). The amount of foreign currency allowed into the country is unlimited, but the full amount must be declared and accounted for upon leaving. It is forbidden to remove Chinese currency, and remaining RMB must be reconverted before leaving the country.

Travelers Checks. Travelers checks usually bring a slightly higher exchange rate than currency. They are accepted from most of

CHINESE CURRENCY (RMB)
EXCHANGE RATES

Country		Buy	Sell
US	$100	171.1	169.6
Argentina	100	7.7	7.7
Belgium	F 100	5.2	5.2
Brazil	100	3.4	3.4
Canada	$100	151.5	151.8
Colombia	100	1.6	1.6
Federal Republic of Germany	DM100	80.6	80.0
France	F 100	36.1	35.8
Hong Kong	$100	37.2	36.9
Italy	L 100,000	196.9	195.4
Japan	Y 100,000	706.6	704.0
Mexico	100	2.5	2.5
Peru	100	.46	.46
Switzerland	F 100	86.2	85.8
UK	L 100	311.7	312.1
Venezuela	100	13.6	13.6

Note: Rates as of March 1978.

the world's leading banks and issuing agencies (as of 1978, notable exceptions were American Express and Citibank checks). A Bank of China check was introduced in 1978 (they are sold at the Bank's branches in Hong Kong). Others negotiable in China include Bank of America, Barclays, Thomas Cook, Lloyds, Midland, National Westminster, Bank of Tokyo, Fuji, Mitsui, Sumitomo, Algemene Bank Nederland, Australia and New Zealand Banking Group, Bank für Gemeinwirtschaft, Banque de Bruxelles, Banque Nationale de Paris, Commercial Bank of Australia, Credit Lyonnais, Deutsche Bank, Hong Kong and Shanghai Banking Corporation, Standard Chartered Bank, and Swiss Bankers. There is no black market in China. Checks and foreign currency should be converted only at branches of the Bank of China (in most hotels) or at a Friendship Store.

It is also possible to arrange for a letter of credit payable to the visitor through the Bank of China. This can be done through most large international banks for a service fee. The procedure is cumbersome, however, and is not recommended except in cases where it might be necessary to transfer some emergency funds to someone already in China. The only bank in the US that has a direct "correspondent" relationship with the Bank of China is the First National Bank of Chicago.

It is usually recommended that the traveler exchange money as needed; this prevents having to contend with a large stack of Chinese notes (the largest denomination, a Y10 note, is worth about US$5.88), and will avoid minor losses from reconversion at the end of the trip.

Postal Service and Telecommunications

China maintains good mail and telecommunications links with the outside world. Telex and phototelegraphic facilities are available for business transactions. Most communications services are available at hotels.

Mail. Postal rates for international mail were sharply increased in 1977. The following is a brief summary of rates (in Chinese yuan):

Postcard	(airmail)	.60
Letter	(airmail)	.70 for first 10 g.
	(surface)	.40 for up to 20 g.
Aerogram		.60
Small packets	(surface)	.60 up to 100 g.
	(airmail)	.60 + .15 for every 10 g. or fraction thereof.

Telephone. Long-distance calls to North America are charged at the rate of Y9.60 (US$5.65) per minute, with a minimum charge of three minutes. A service charge of Y4 (US$2.35) is made on all calls, whether or not completed. Charges may be reversed to most countries. Long-distance calls may be booked at hotel service desks and usually take 5-15 minutes to be completed.

Cable. Telegram rates to overseas destinations vary considerably from country to country, but generally fall within Y1.20-1.50 per word. The per-word charge to the US is Y1.30 ($0.76). The rate is doubled for "express" (four-hour) delivery and is halved for "regular cable" (night letter). Because of the high cable rates, it may be worth considering a phone call in some instances.

Telex. Telex facilities are available at main and branch post offices in large cities. Only three hotels have telex: the Chin Chiang

Hotel in Shanghai and the Tung Fang and Bai Yun in Kwangchow. Patrons must punch their own tapes. Rates to all overseas destinations, excluding Hong Kong, are Y8.40 ($4.94) per minute, with a minimum three-minute charge.

Incoming Correspondence. Delivery of mail from North America generally takes a week to ten days. For most tours, it is thus impractical to request mail from home. Since exact daily itineraries and hotels are rarely known prior to arrival in China, mail should not be addressed to hotels or cities. To facilitate such contacts the proper address to use is:

Name of Individual, Name of Group, c/o Host Organization (e.g., China International Travel Service), Peking, People's Republic of China.

Cables can reach the visitor in the same manner (the cable address of China International Travel Service is its Chinese name: LUXING-SHE). Every effort is made to deliver cables promptly. For business travelers spending some time in one place, it is advantageous to register a cable address (for a small fee).

Incoming telephone calls are connected by an overseas operator. Callers should instruct the operator to contact the host organization in Peking in order to locate the delegation and the individual being sought. This procedure can be remarkably efficient—one party received a phone call from the US in less than three hours on a Sunday night, even though they were on an "unscheduled" side trip to a small resort hotel in central China.

Health

Many visitors have commented on the extraordinary concern shown by the Chinese for their guests' health and have praised the excellent care provided by Chinese hospitals and medical personnel. Medical services are available to visitors at hospitals and local clinics in all major cities and in the countryside. There is clearly great interest in doing everything possible in terms of both preventive measures and treatment.

The most common maladies afflicting travelers in China are respiratory problems such as head colds, bronchial conditions, and sore throats. Diarrhea may also be a problem, and appropriate remedies should be taken along on the prior advice of a physician. Visitors should be sure to pack ample supplies of prescribed medications, since many prescriptions may be difficult to obtain in China.

Sanitary conditions are generally excellent. Tap water is not potable in China, even in large cities. Hotel rooms are supplied with boiled water in thermos bottles or carafes. Ice is made from purified water and local beverages are safe. Restaurants take the sensitivity of their foreign guests' stomachs into account, and even meals prepared on rural communes will have been carefully supervised.

Tour guides are extremely solicitous about health problems, and at first sign of illness will recommend seeing a doctor.

Hospitals. Should an illness require hospitalization, both Western and Chinese medicines are available. Visitors will be given their choice of treatment (it is in no case advisable, however, to go to China with the expectation of getting long-standing rheumatism or gall bladder disorders cured by herbs or acupuncture). The Chinese do not have RH-negative blood, and their blood banks do not store it. Persons with this blood-type should consult their physician before departing for China.

In case of serious illness, it is possible to have relatives summoned, and the Chinese will facilitate special invitations, visa clearance, and other necessary arrangements. At the same time, one should notify one's embassy (or, for US citizens, the Liaison Office) in Peking.

Some visitors may be put off by what may appear to be primitive medical facilities. There are no luxury hospitals in China, no carpeted waiting rooms, and few examples of the complex diagnostic equipment found in the West. Considering the barrier of language (although an interpreter will always come along to help) and the strange surroundings, it is natural to feel uncomfortable. Such qualms are unfounded, however, since Chinese physicians are well trained and their diagnostic techniques sophisticated, time-honored, and judicious.

Hotel Accommodations

For most travelers, hotel accommodations are prearranged by CITS or other host organizations. Hotels in China generally meet first-class international standards, with good service. Rates and facilities vary somewhat from city to city, but most hotels that serve foreigners are equipped with similar amenities.

Room Amenities. Hotel rooms in China are simple and functional, but comfortable. They generally contain twin beds, a desk, easy chair, bureau, and bathroom. A carafe of preboiled drinking water is provided, as is a thermos of hot water for tea. Lighting is sometimes inadequate, especially for reading or writing at night, and travelers may wish to pack high-wattage bulbs for the trip.

Services. Most hotels have postal, banking, and telegraph and cable facilities on the premises. Hotel shops sell snacks, general travel items, and handicrafts. Room service is available. In addition, each residence floor has a service counter which will handle laundry and dry cleaning (laundry normally takes one day, dry cleaning two) and book long-distance telephone calls. Service counters also sell mineral water, beer, and Chinese liquor. Most hotels are now equipped to supply ice.

Food

Of the world's two great cuisines, the Chinese is as varied as, and, in fact, much older in tradition than the French. Chinese chefs are masters at creating culinary triumphs from the barest necessities. Indeed, some of the most prized delicacies are said to have been concocted during times of famine—many from substances never before considered edible. The manner of serving even the simplest dishes at once appeals to the eye, the sense of smell, and the palate.

Hotel Dining. Generally speaking, most tour groups and visiting delegations take all of their meals at the hotels (except for welcoming banquets). Meals are served at predesignated times (usually 8, 12, and 6), at preassigned tables, and from a menu preselected by the

A Restaurant Menu

hotel cooks. Unless special requests are made, breakfast will be Western style (eggs, toast, jam, coffee, a cake or pastry); lunch and dinner are Chinese. It is usually póssible to order a Chinese-style breakfast a day in advance, and if enough people to fill a table (eight or ten) require it. The hotel dining rooms will also be glad to serve Western food for lunch and dinner, again if the request is made well ahead of time and if enough persons in a group ask for it. It is not possible to order individually prepared dishes, although the Chinese will prepare special meals for visitors with special dietary requirements. Most beverages, including beer, are considered part of the meal, the cost of which is included in the tour package.

Restaurants. Although it will entail an additional expense, eating at a local restaurant is highly recommended, both for its atmosphere as well as for noticeable improvements in the quality and variety of food. Excursions can be arranged by forming a group and making reservations through a tour escort, the main service desk at the hotel, or at the restaurant itself (this usually requires a Chinese-speaking person). The custom is to establish a price range (Y10-15 per person is standard) and make advance requests for special dishes.

Banquets. It has been customary for the host organization in China to give a welcoming dinner in honor of visiting groups or delegations. Depending on the protocol required, the dinner can be an elaborate banquet—complete with formal invitations and a detailed seating plan—or a simpler affair. In both cases, many of the same procedures apply.

All meals in China—including banquets—start at the announced time. Tardiness is considered rude. Formal dinners are timed to last about an hour and a half. Arriving guests are usually ushered into an anteroom and offered tea, hot towels, and about 10 to 15 minutes of light conversation with the hosts. The principal host will then signal that dinner is ready, and guests will be seated according to protocol. The host will preside, sitting at a head table (Chinese tradition dictates that the seat of honor faces the door), with the highest ranking guests (i.e., the delegation's leaders) arranged to his left and right. It is customary for hosts to serve guests with special chopsticks and implements.

A typical setting will include a small plate, a pair of chopsticks resting on a holder (forks and knives are always available), and three glasses: for beer or soft drinks, wine, and the customary *mao t'ai* (a fiery 140° proof liquor). Dishes are served in sequence, starting with cold appetizers and continuing to ten courses and beyond. A well-balanced meal will contain, at a minimum, the five basic tastes of Chinese cuisine (acid, hot, bitter, sweet, and salt). Dishes alternate between crisp and tender, dry and thickly sauced. Soup usually concludes the main courses; in the south, fried rice or noodles come last. Dessert is usually fresh fruit with pastries.

It is polite to eat (or at least appear to eat) a bit of each dish served, pacing oneself through the course of the meal. In formal settings, it is impolite to drink alcohol alone, and thus toasts are usually offered either among neighbors or to the table as a whole. At banquets, it is appropriate to offer toasts to the entire assemblage. The host usually begins the toasts after the first course. The leader of the visiting group follows with his toast after a few courses. Excessive toasting should be avoided, however. Inebriation is frowned upon. Individual restaurant recommendations and local dishes are discussed in the sections on individual cities.

Entertainment

Two themes dominate cultural life in the PRC: the pervasive use of art forms as a means of political education, and the encouragement of broad participation in cultural activities by all segments of the population—from school children to factory workers to farmers. In the course of most China tours, visitors will have a chance to attend a variety of cultural performances, most of which will have some set of political messages at their core (acrobatic performances are an exception to this rule). In this respect, culture is no different from all other forms of collective activity in today's China. Art may serve to promote enjoyment, excitement, and good feelings among its practitioners and observers. But, more importantly, it must seek to make a specific and concrete contribution to the goals of nation-building.

Approached in this context, an evening's entertainment in China can provide a rewarding cross-cultural experience for foreign visitors. As is their intent, these performances offer a means for better comprehending central values in PRC society. Not incidentally, many of these bright, exuberant displays also succeed delightfully as entertainment.

Performing Arts. A wide range of performing-art genres are practiced in today's China. In addition to their general stress on political themes, most presentations—be they in the form of opera, dance, film, or theater—are marked by a high degree of stylization (e.g., lots of posturing and broad gestures) and by an outward freshness and enthusiasm conveyed by the performers. In addition, visitors must be cautioned that most cultural presentations in China are not known for their brevity.

Peking Opera, probably the best-known of China's traditional art forms, was undergoing a revival in the late 1970s. Operas with both classical and modern themes were being performed in great profusion and variety throughout the country. Many regions in China have developed their own operatic styles. For most, however, plots can be obscure and intricate; if possible, story-lines should be consulted and sorted out before the performance. Ballets such as *The White-Haired Girl* and *Red Detachment of Women* are among the modern classics of this genre, which combines dance, choral singing, and visual effects in a manner designed to engulf the senses. Similarly, Chinese theater makes extravagant use of action, color, and forthright emotion. Acrobatic performances are now common to most tourist itineraries. Here, subtle skill and visual impact are stressed over displays that court bodily danger.

Shopping

The Chinese are continually nonplussed by the Westener's penchant for shopping, but are certain to arrange at least one group visit to the local Friendship Store or department store so that visitors may exercise their curious compulsions. China is not a consumer society and there is no equivalent of Fifth Avenue in New York, the Ginza in Tokyo, or the Champs Elysées in Paris. The emphasis in Chinese products is on the everyday and the practical, with the notable exception of some splendid handicrafts. The tourist will find that basic items are inexpensive, but that there are few bargains, even among such common "Chinese" items as jade, jewelry, and antiques. In fact, some "luxury" goods may be cheaper and available in wider varieties in Hong Kong. Other shopping hints will be found in individual shopping sections in the city itineraries.

Friendship Stores. Friendship Stores have been established in the major cities specifically to sell export items to foreign visitors. Thus, they offer many products that do not circulate in the local economy (i.e., exclusive silks, jewelry, or intricate lacquerware). Guides will encourage visitors to do most of their shopping in these stores.

Other advantages include sales personnel who speak foreign languages, a wide selection of merchandise, and the best quality range available for most items. Friendship Stores have uncrowded counters, facilities for packing and shipping large items home (in Peking), and the helpful presence of tour guides. In nearly all cases, the prices of items will be the same as in regular stores.

However, the very attributes of Friendship Stores can also be disadvantages: visitors are deprived of the experience of mingling with Chinese shoppers. Also, mundane items that may be unusual outside of China are not carried in the Friendship Stores (for example, books, posters, and crockery).

If possible, both types of shopping should be tried. Friendship Stores are located in Peking (the largest and best-supplied), Shanghai, and Kwangchow, and are being added in scaled-down versions in many other cities.

Local Stores. There are usually several major shopping areas in most cities visited, many close to the hotel. The best approach is to go out and explore them on your own. Prices are almost always marked. If communication becomes difficult, Chinese shopkeepers will usually write out the price (in Arabic numerals) on a slip of paper. Veteran travelers will note the absence of inflation in China. Prices are set by the state and will not vary from store to store. (A can of "Ma Ling" peanuts has been Y1.43 for the past five years, no matter where in China it was seen.) There is absolutely no bargaining.

The Chinese are scrupulously honest. If visitors can't figure out the exact payment from the assortment of bills and coins, the sales staff will offer to fish out the correct amount. Receipts are always provided and should be kept.

Except in Friendship Stores, a number of items are rationed: cigarettes, cottons, and "luxury" fabrics such as silk. Local department stores or clothing shops abide strictly by these rules. If one is "waved off" from an item, offense should not be taken; it simply means ration coupons are required (in some cases, purchase of such items can be arranged with the help of the Chinese tour escort, but not without some difficulty).

There is another aspect of shopping to keep in mind, especially in areas where foreign visits are less frequent. Expect to be stared at (in a friendly way) and even followed. This should not be interpreted as hostility or a discourtesy but merely as an expression of curiosity and interest. Under such circumstances, it's best to smile and continue on.

Antiques. Persons who come to China expecting to find an antique-buyers paradise are likely to be disappointed. First, antiques are sold only in licensed shops in Peking, Kwangchow, Wuhsi, Kweilin, and a few other cities. Second, authorities have restricted sale of any item older than 150 years. They regulate what is purchased by marking it with a special red wax seal and requiring a special customs declaration form, issued at the time of purchase. Third, the Chinese are well aware of the international market prices of antiques and charge accordingly; there simply are no bargains left. Finally, the stores—especially in Kwangchow and Peking—have been thoroughly "picked over" during the past several years as visitors to China have increased in number. This is not to say that the pursuit itself will not be rewarding. The availability of many unusual "non-antiques"—jewelry, ceramics, and even paintings—may make the venture worthwhile.

Items Recommended for Purchase. Individual taste will always dictate what is a good buy and what isn't, though the following indicates some of the most popular items bought in China over the past years and the best places to get them:

Rugs (Peking)
Ceramics (Kwangchow, Changsha)
Ivory (Kwangchow, Peking) (note: as products from
  endangered species, illegal for US import)
Clay figurines (Peking, Wuhsi, Kwangchow)
Cloisonné, lacquer ware (Peking, Shanghai)
Jewelry, including jade (Peking, Shanghai, Kwangchow)
Silk (Hangchow, Soochow, Wuhsi, Shanghai)
Embroidery (Changsha, Soochow)
Furs and suedes (Peking, Shenyang)
Scroll paintings (Peking, Shanghai)
Woodblock prints and stone rubbings (Peking only)
Papercuts (everywhere)
Mao t'ai and other liquors (everywhere—beware, *mao t'ai*
  bottles will leak through their seals.)

Other items to look for: chops (signature seals); postage stamp sets; miniature carvings in stone, cork, or wood; sandalwood fans; brushes and art supplies; knives; books; posters; and acupuncture dolls. Always look for the unusual: in Shanghai and Kwangchow, cold cream comes packaged in a charming double sea shell and is sold for about 30 fen ($0.18).

Import Restrictions. It is worth checking import restrictions before buying expensive items (rugs, jade, antiques). This is especially so for the US, where Chinese imports are subject to the discriminatory "Column 2" duties (since the PRC has not been granted "most-favored-nation" status). This means that the US duty on almost all items automatically doubles. A piece of made-up silver jewelry, for example, is dutiable at 110% of its value.

Selected Foreign Diplomatic Missions in Peking

Australia. 41 San Li Tun (tel: 522331).

Austria. Jian Guo Men Wai, Hsiu, Shui Nan Chieh, 5 (tel: 522061 or 522063).

Belgium. 34 San Li Tun (tel: 521736-38).

Canada. 16 San Li Tun (tel: 521475).

Chile. 22 San Li Tun (tel: 521287).

Denmark. San Li Tun (tel: 522431).

Federal Republic of Germany. Diplomatic Office Building, 39 San Li Tun (tel: 521161-65).

Finland. 3 Kwang Hua Road (tel: 521817).

France. 10 San Li Tun (tel: 521331-35).

Greece. 19 Kwang Hua Road (tel: 522250).

Italy. Diplomatic Office Building, Apt. No. 1-71/72, Entrance No. 1, San Li Tun (tel: 522131).

Japan. 48 San Li Tun (tel: 522055).

Mexico. Diplomatic Office Building 2, 72; 29 San Li Tun (tel: 522055, 521396, 522070).

Netherlands. 2 San Li Tun (tel: 521731).

New Zealand. No. 1 Building, No. 2 Street, East Temple of the Sun (tel: 522731).

Norway. 11 San Li Tun (tel: 552262).

Peru. 2-82 San Li Tun (tel: 522178, 522005, 521480).

Spain. Building 45, San Li Tun (tel: 521436-39).

Sweden. 22 San Li Tun (tel: 521770, 521252).

Switzerland. 25 Tung An Men Nan Chieh (tel: 551914, 551259).

United Kingdom. 5 Hua Chien Kuo Men Wai (tel: 521961-64).

United States (Liaison Office). 17 Kwang Hua Road (tel: 522033).

GETTING AROUND IN CHINA

Most travel between the major cities of China is by air. Shorter inter-city excursions are by train. With the exception of commercial travel-ers, foreign visitors will not have to buy their own tickets for air or train travel; the host organization handles all reservations, ticket pur-chases, and appropriate clearances with the public security bureau (a "foreigners check post" is set up at all major airports and train sta-tions).

Domestic Air Travel. The Chinese airline, the Civil Aviation Ad-ministration of China (CAAC), has expanded its services greatly over the past several years. Its nine international routes total 40,000 km. (24,840 mi.), covering all continents (except the Western Hemi-sphere). Domestically, CAAC has 100 routes totaling 147,543 km. (91,624 mi.) and linking 80 different cities with the capital, Peking. CAAC uses an array of jet aircraft—Boeing 707s, British Tridents, and Soviet Ilyushins—between the three major cities of Peking, Shanghai, and Kwangchow as well as between other points. Propel-ler planes such as the Soviet Antonov are used between small- and in-termediate-sized cities.

Air travel in China has become increasingly more comfortable (the Soviet planes are exceptions, with their notorious lack of leg room) and schedules more convenient. Flights are often crowded, mainly with officials, People's Liberation Army personnel, and foreigners. All passengers are limited to 30 kilos (66 pounds) baggage allowance in first class, 20 kilos (44 pounds) in economy class. Excess baggage charges amount to 1% of the applicable one-way fare, mak-ing the charge for an additional kilo (2.2 lbs) on the Peking to Kwangchow sector, Y2.44 ($1.44).

Airports, whether new or old, are spartan, with vacant, unadorn-ed waiting rooms. Each airport usually has a small retail shop (sell-ing regional specialties) and a restaurant. The largest air terminal facility in China is expected to be opened in Peking in 1978. Shang-hai has the second largest. Some airports also serve as military bases, especially in the interior of China. Photography is not allowed aboard an airplane, either in the air or while taxiing.

CAAC serves meals on its longer flights, although these do not en-joy a favorable reputation. On shorter flights, fruit or pastries, ac-companied by tea, are often served. Liquor is not served, but cigarettes, lapel pins, candy, gum, and address books are handed out as souvenirs of the flight.

DISTANCE BETWEEN MAIN TOURIST CITIES

Shortest Railway Distance
1,000 = kilometers
621 = miles

	Peking	Shanghai	Tientsin	Kwangchow	Changsha	Nanking	Hangchow	Tsingtao	Sian	Chengchow
Shanghai	1,462 / 908									
Tsientsin	137 / 85	1,325 / 824								
Kwangchow	2,324 / 1,445	1,822 / 1,132	2,461 / 1,530							
Changsha	1,587 / 986	1,187 / 738	1,724 / 1,071	737 / 458						
Nanking	1,157 / 719	305 / 190	1,020 / 634	2,127 / 1,322	1,492 / 927					
Hangchow	1,651 / 1,026	189 / 118	1,514 / 941	1,633 / 1,015	998 / 620	494 / 307				
Tsingtao	887 / 551	1,361 / 846	750 / 466	2,688 / 1,671	1,951 / 1,213	1,056 / 656	1,550 / 963			
Sian	1,165 / 724	1,511 / 939	1,302 / 809	2,140 / 1,330	1,403 / 872	1,206 / 750	1,700 / 1,006	1,570 / 976		
Chengchow	695 / 432	1,000 / 622	832 / 517	1,029 / 1,012	892 / 554	695 / 432	1,189 / 739	1,059 / 658	511 / 318	
Shenyang	841 / 523	2,029 / 1,261	704 / 438	3,165 / 1,967	2,428 / 1,509	1,724 / 1,071	2,218 / 1,379	1,454 / 904	2,006 / 1,247	1,536 / 955

Train Travel. Train travel is by far the most enjoyable way to see China, since it is not only comfortable, but affords an excellent view of the Chinese countryside. Fares are also considerably lower than air travel.

The Chinese divide their trains into "hard seat" and "soft seat" compartments, with the latter reserved for foreigners and high-ranking Chinese such as army personnel and government officials. On long-distance trains there are sleeping coaches reminiscent of European trains, accommodating 32 passengers—four each in eight separate compartments, each with its own bunks, wood-paneled walls, fan, curtains, and a small potted plant. Such trains also have dining cars (as does the Kwangchow-to-Hong Kong train).

Chinese trains invariably run on time. A long, ringing bell is the signal for departure. As the train pulls out of the station, it is accompanied by martial music carried over loudspeakers in each compartment or coach. The music continues sporadically during the trip—dining, conversation, even slumber are frequently interrupted by loudspeaker announcements of stops, time, news reports, and interludes of music. If the traveler prefers, it is possibile to turn off the speaker system, either in the individual compartments where the switch is located under the table, or near the door at the end of each car. Carriages are meticulously serviced by attendants, who regularly mop the floors, clean woodwork, serve tea and other beverages (unlike airplanes, trains serve beer and, occasionally, wine), and turn the loudspeakers back on.

Urban Transport. Within cities, visitors are conveyed by bus, private car, or taxi. High-ranking visitors are often chauffered in "Shanghai" sedans, while heads of state or guests of ministries may be provided with the larger and more elegant "Hung Ch'i" (Red Flag) limousine.

Tour groups usually travel on 25-passenger Chinese buses or 16-seat Japanese minibuses. (Kwangchow now uses Romanian "Icarus" tour buses for large groups.) Although newer models are perfectly comfortable, none are air-conditioned. Older vehicles are less satisfactory, especially on long rides such as to the Great Wall (a two-hour journey). Older buses are gradually being phased out, however.

Taxi fleets (usually Toyotas) serve the major hotels in the cities of Peking, Shanghai, and Kwangchow. Fares are computed on a formula incorporating both time and distance. For a fixed hourly rate, the driver will wait while the visitor goes about business or sightseeing; an afternoon's excursion can cost US$10-15. Some travelers regard

Chinese taxis as not only convenient but also as something of an adventure, especially at night when vehicles in China dart through the streets without lights (used only as warning signals). Taxi dispatchers are situated in the lobbies of hotels. Store or restaurant staff will help summon one on request.

Travel on China's efficient and inexpensive urban bus and trolley systems is possible but somewhat complicated. Ticket prices are based on distances traveled, making it vital to know one's final destination. This requires some knowledge of Chinese or the services of an interpreter. For those able to read Chinese there are convenient route maps at most major stops. Buses are usually crowded, but people are extremely courteous to foreigners and it is not unusual for a young Westerner to be offered a seat by an elderly Chinese.

There are at present no passenger ships that travel between the major ports of China (although the introduction of a coastal tourist ship was being discussed in 1977). Ferries cross major rivers, such as the Whangpoo in Shanghai or the Pearl in Kwangchow. Such rides are recommended in leisure time, since they may allow exploration of areas not often visited. Fares are usually less than 10 fen (US$0.05).

THE GROUP TRAVEL EXPERIENCE

All visits to China are directly coordinated by the host organization that provided initial authorization for the trip. Upon arrival, the host organization assumes all responsibility for domestic travel and accommodations.

General tour groups, including friendship groups and study tours, will be accompanied by representatives from the China International Travel Service (CITS). Professional groups will be hosted by representatives of their counterpart organization in China. Official, government-hosted delegations will be accompanied by a ranking member of the host organization. This person fulfills both protocol and escort functions, and works closely with the visiting group's leader. Business representatives, by contrast, are left much more to their own devices, mainly since they do not usually travel from city to city. Business persons are expected to arrange appointments by themselves, although the Chinese may provide escorts for first-time visitors to Peking or Shanghai. If a business representative's schedule allows for sightseeing or for travel between cities, an escort and/or interpreter from the appropriate Chinese trade corporation can be provided on request.

Arrival. A representative of the host organization will be on hand to welcome visitors upon their arrival in China. He or she is likely to accompany the group throughout its stay in the PRC. These personnel serve as escorts, guides, and interpreters, and will have themselves made all prior arrangements for the tour. Upon arrival at the preassigned hotel, people may go directly to their rooms (also preassigned). Usually, a meeting with the host is arranged shortly thereafter to discuss the proposed itinerary and work out details of the stay. Initial meetings with host representatives are important. They serve to mutually acquaint escorts and guests, work out the itinerary, and generally set the tone for the visit. After guests are formally welcomed to China, a schedule is proposed. The Chinese usually prearrange trips in accordance with the interests of the group as expressed in their initial tour application. The schedule should be gone over in detail since it will be nearly impossible to make changes afterwards, especially those that involve alterations of travel dates between cities or of appointments at particular institutions. Likewise, suggestions for splitting up into subgroups are rarely accommodated.

Adjustments in the tone and organization of tours are made for political groups, friendship tours, general study trips, professionals, and commercial visitors. Each type is handled according to a different set of expectations. Thus, a business representative who continually quotes Chairman Mao may be looked upon with curiosity. The Chinese zeal for categorization of tour groups is well intentioned, the point being to make the sojourn in China as relevant as possible to the group's major interests. Inevitably, however, groups of more diverse makeup may find themselves being unduly stereotyped.

Group Leaders. The Chinese are sensitive to leadership responsibilites and will expect their guests to appoint a group leader. Leaders of foreign groups are treated with some deference. For their part, leaders are expected to assume responsibility for introductions at the places visited and to act as intermediaries for complaints and suggestions. Most delegations also select a "secretary" who can serve as the first point of contact with Chinese personnel in making room assignments or working out schedule details.

Escort Procedures. A pattern of organization becomes apparent during the first few days of a stay in China. Escorts and interpreters will meet with the group at the outset of any planned activity, make the introductions at the institutions or sites visited, and help with any problems—from protocol to travel, from shopping to laundry—that may arise.

A group may not always be in the company of the same guide, since each factory, school, museum, park, or other site maintains personnel who specialize in meeting "foreign friends." There will, however, be at least one interpreter assigned to the group at all times. Most delegations have found translators to be quite competent. These persons have a particularly grueling task, since they bear the major burden of making Chinese society comprehensible to the foreigner. Interpreters are called upon to translate briefings, speeches, signs, and conversations for many hours each day, often after having visited the same institution a number of times.

Free time between scheduled appointments can be used for shopping, walking around, or other leisure activities. Such excursions do not require an official escort.

On-Site Briefings. When visiting a factory, school, commune, or other institution, the tour group or delegation is normally escorted to a room to have tea and receive a briefing from a "leading member" of the institution. Remarks usually take note of changes since the revolution, the effect of the current policy line, and general statistics. Guests are usually invited to ask questions as they tour the site. If time allows, the group may return to the briefing room for further follow-up.

Questioning is always encouraged, but visitors should be sensitive about the style of questions and the areas probed. Unanswered questions should not be pursued beyond the bounds of courtesy. Reticence on the part of a spokesman should not be taken as a sign of evasion or deception. From the Chinese standpoint, briefings serve to fill a narrow, specific context. Most Chinese in this situation are not given to extemporizing and, lacking information or the authority to give a complete answer, they will prefer to give none. The Chinese generally prefer to take all questions at once, answering them in as much detail as time and discretion allow. While this method works fairly well with larger tour groups, smaller delegations may prefer to ask their questions one at a time so that appropriate follow-up inquiries can be made.

General Behavior and Decorum

Under the special conditions imposed by escorted group travel, visitors should seek to exercise courtesy and patience. It is always best to try to relax and "flow" with the visit. A willingness to experience China on its own terms will result in a more satisfying visit, whether its purpose be business or general travel. The accumulated experience of recent visitors has produced some guidelines that will facilitate relationships.

General Conduct. The Chinese expect their guests to behave as representatives of their own society and are respectful of cultural and national differences. Visitors should act themselves, and feel free to speak openly about differing political, economic, religious, or social beliefs. Spirited disagreements, however, should not be allowed to degenerate into remarks that are disrespectful towards aspects of Chinese society or particularly towards its leaders.

While Western manners need not be abandoned in China, some restraint is advisable. The Chinese do not appreciate a "hail fellow, well met" style and are sparing in their use of direct physical contact. A courteous handshake is acceptable. As one gets to know the Chinese, greater familiarity becomes possible. Public displays of affection among members of visiting groups are also regarded as unseemly. Likewise, visitors should attempt to keep a pleasant demeanor and not show hostility or anger in public either towards the Chinese or fellow group members.

Norms of etiquette in the PRC do not differentiate between men and women, and members of both sexes are treated equally.

Terminology. Terms for China in Western usage such as "Red China," "Mainland China," or "Communist China" may cause offense, as may references to Taiwan as the "Republic of China" or "Free China." The preferred name for China is the People's Republic of China or, simply, China.

Punctuality and Protocol. Punctuality is expected for all business and social appointments. Except in extenuating circumstances, all planned activities and meetings should be attended. This is as important for general visitors as for business representatives. Even the most mundane arrangements may have required considerable preparation on the part of the Chinese.

Tour groups and delegations visiting an institution (or arriving at a negotiating session) should be cognizant of protocol requirements. The leader or senior member of the party should enter first since the Chinese will have lined up their hosts in protocol order. It is also appropriate to introduce group members individually after the Chinese have made their own introductions.

Voicing Complaints. Individuals should not be criticized or chastised openly. If complaints about arrangements must be raised, they should be broached first in private with an escort or interpreter.

For example, if a group visits a commune and is advised that it is "inconvenient" to tour the local hospital, members should not insist on being taken there, even if they have just walked by it. When there is an opportunity, it may be mentioned in friendly terms that the group has a special interest in hospitals and it hopes there may be another opportunity to visit one. If, indeed, another opportunity is possible, it will usually be granted.

Expressing Gratitude. Tipping, whether in cash or gifts, is strictly forbidden in the PRC. The only appropriate gesture, in the case of official or special-interest delegations, is to arrange a return banquet for the host organization (at the end of the trip) and to present the host organization with a collective gift, such as plaques, technical or scientific books, and the like. Tour groups and delegations sometimes take lapel pins, postcards, small flags, or other tokens, from home. These can be presented to a school, commune, factory, or other collective entity. Instant pictures are popular. It is thought unseemly for business people to present gifts in China. They are likely to be instantly returned, to great mutual embarrassment.

The Chinese have a justified reputation for honesty. They will endeavor to return any items that have been misplaced, including some that have been intentionally discarded or left behind. If one wishes to dispose of belongings such as worn clothing or books, they may be given directly to workers at the service desk, with an explanation that the items are no longer needed and may be disposed of.

The China Itinerary

TRAVEL
REGIONS

- NORTH
- EAST
- CENTRAL
- SOUTH

NORTH CHINA

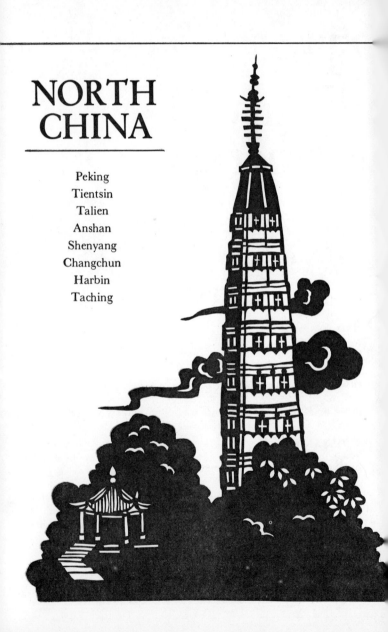

Peking

北
京

northern capital
Pinyin Spelling: Beijing ("bay-jing")

Although Peking has been the capital of China for the better part of the past 700 years, its role has never been as dominant as it is today. It is at once the seat of the strongest central government in China's history, and the political, administrative, communications, and cultural hub of the People's Republic of China. The city is one of China's three centrally-administered municipalities (Shanghai and Tientsin are the other two).

Peking occupies 17,800 sq.km. (6,870 sq.mi.) at the northwest edge of the great North China Plain. Its latitude is approximately that of Philadelphia or Madrid. The municipality as a whole has a population of about 7,570,000, ranking it among the world's ten largest cities. Nearly half of the population resides outside of the urban nucleus in the several thousand square miles of rural area that have been annexed to the municipality.

Peking today has retained many facets of its antiquity, but has subordinated them to intensive urban development. Most of the old walled town in the heart of the city (including its basic street plan) dates to before the 16th century, but today the venerable Gate of Heavenly Peace faces the Monument to the People's Heroes and the MaoTse-tung Memorial Hall. The old city walls have been torn down, their lines now traced by a circumferential subway surmounted by 15-story apartment buildings.

Peking has no central business district, just a series of market areas connected by wide boulevards. As a result, there is no center-oriented rush hour. Modern factories have been built to the southwest to avoid adding industrial fumes to the prevailing dust-bearing north-westerly winds. Government office buildings are scattered in various sections of town. Thus, the center of Peking tends to convey a rather empty feeling. The impression is heightened by the old-style residential areas (called *hu-tungs*) where grey stone dwellings huddle inside long walls that blankly frame the narrow streets and alleyways.

Yet there is no mistaking the central importance of Peking: even clocks in the most remote corners of the country set their time to Peking's. The key national Party and government newspapers are printed here, the national political congresses take place here, and all of China's major railway lines and air routes radiate from the city. Unquestionably, standing at the Gate of Heavenly Peace and facing Tien An Men Square, the visitor senses proximity to the heart of China.

An ideal time of year to visit Peking is late September and early October, after the summer rains have lost their intensity. During this short period, Peking remains green and cool. It then undergoes an abrupt transition into a cold winter when temperatures often drop below freezing. By late winter, the dry earth is fanned by brisk northern winds that swirl dust everywhere. Most summers are characterized by spells of oppressive heat, interrupted by periods of heavy rainfall; temperatures may occasionally exceed 38° C (100° F). July is the rainy season, when almost 40% of the total annual precipitation occurs, often in the form of violent thunderstorms.

Peking in History

A skull of "Peking man" said to be over 500,000 years old gives evidence that the Peking region had been occupied in prehistoric times, indeed as far back as the very dawn of human evolution. Archeological records of a town date to 3,000 years ago. At that time, during the Chou Dynasty, Peking was a small village on the edge of the Yang Tung River (12 miles southwest of Tien An Men). It served as a commercial link between the mountains of the north and the fertile plains to the south.

During the Warring States period, Peking was known as "Chi" (meaning "reed"). With the building of the Great Wall under the Ch'in Dynasty in the 3rd century BC, the town began to grow and prosper, and continued to expand under both the Han and T'ang Dynasties. In 608 AD, the Emperor Yang Ti constructed a canal from the Yellow River to the Peking area in order to supply his armies in their campaigns against Korea; this was the start of the Grand Canal. During a period of turmoil in the 10th century, when northern tribes held power over China (Five Dynasties), the town lost its strategic importance. In fact, it at one point served as the southern capital of the Khitan people (Khitan, or Khitai, is the origin of "Cathay," the name for China used in Medieval Europe).

The Mongols captured the town in 1122 AD. They renamed it Chung Tu (Central Capital) and enlarged it, retaining the square layout but adding walls and gates. During the early 13th century, the city was destroyed in a struggle between warring factions. It was not until the Mongol ruler Kublai Khan established himself there in 1267 —renaming it Ta Tu (Great Capital)— that the town was rebuilt and the basic plan that still dominates present-day Peking laid out. Life in the city during its Mongol renaissance (Yuan Dynasty, 1260-1365) was grandiloquently described by Marco Polo, who visited Peking in 1275.

When the Mongols gave way to the Ming Dynasty, they left behind a ruined capital city. The first Ming emperor established his capital in Nanking, but Emperor Yung Lo (1403-24) re-established the imperial capital at Peking in 1421. New city walls were constructed, extending to a height of 40 feet and forming a 14-mile battlement around the city. There were four main gates, each protected by an outer portal. (At present, only the north and south gates remain standing; urban renewal under the present government has necessitated removal of the others.) The Imperial Palace was built during the Ming era, adding an element of architectural grandeur to an otherwise bleak, unprepossessing setting.

At the end of the Ming Dynasty (1644), Peking fell under the con-

The Great Wall

trol of bandits (prompting the last emperor to hang himself). The invading Manchus inflicted further havoc on the city, looting and burning. During their subsequent long rule (Ch'ing Dynasty, 1644-1912), these non-Han conquerors undertook to rebuild the monuments to Chinese imperial power that their linear predecessors had sought to destroy.

The Manchus began to allow foreigners to travel north of Kwangchow (Canton) to visit the emperor's court. By the 19th century, a sizable community of non-Chinese were living in Peking. Ultimately, foreigners became a factor in the city's deterioration. At the end of the Opium War, Western troops forced the emperor to flee, burning part of the city and wresting residential concessions (the old-French legation was just south of the present-day location of the Peking Hotel).

In 1900, the Boxers (a Chinese secret society) tried to expel the foreigners and restore the previous luster of the empire, but to no avail. During the subsequent two decades, Peking remained the focal point of nationalist sentiment (see below). In 1928, it was renamed Peip'ing (Northern Peace) by the Kuomintang government, which in turn established its capital at Nanking.

On July 7, 1937, a clash between Japanese and Chinese troops led to the "North China Incident," signaling the start of a general state of war in China that lasted until 1949. During much of this period, Peking was occupied by Japanese forces, although its strategic and political importance had been largely drained by domestic events of the previous two decades.

Peking's Role in the Revolution. The roots of the modern revolutionary movement in Peking can be traced to the invasion of the city by 17,000 British and French troops in 1860, an event that ushered in five decades of Western expansionism and hastened the erosion of the imperial dynastic system. Russians, British, French, Americans, and Japanese all vied for influence at the imperial court, which they alternately sought to prop up and force terms upon.

Various reform movements were adopted by the Chinese government to try to recapture its lost strength. The most daring effort came in 1898 when a group of ministers tried to forestall China's rapid deterioration by modernizing the government, forming a parliament, and building up the armed forces. The reform movement failed, however, bringing to power more extreme factions, whose rallying cry became "Expel the barbarian!" The opposition found an effective political and military ally in the Boxers, a secret society founded in the late 18th century on the premise of fomenting popular rebellion against imperial reign. But the Boxers quickly narrowed their emphasis to an anti-foreign thrust and entered into a dubious alliance with the imperial government. The Boxer rebellion of 1900 ended disastrously, signaling the final death-throes of the old society.

The overthrow of the dynastic system by Sun Yat-sen's revolution of 1911 led to the first attempts to lay the foundations for a modern nation. A new government was subsequently established in Peking by Yuan Shih-k'ai (who had usurped Sun's position). But chaos continued to reign. Factionalism, the rise of warlords in different regions of China, and the continuing threat posed by foreign powers led to greater instability. Lingering traditional values could no longer cope with the new forces of social and political change that were welling up. The clearest and most compelling response to this state of confusion was provided by students whose strident calls for nationalism quickly won wide attention and support. On May 4, 1919, some 300,000 youths rallied in the capital to denounce the weakness of the central government's response to the Japanese seizure of Shantung in 1914 and to Japan's "21 Demands" of 1915. The students endorsed a manifesto that concluded:

China's territory may be conquered but it cannot be given away. The Chinese people may be massacred but they will not surrender. Our country is about to be annihilated. Up, brethren!

The May 4th demonstration was among the most important political events in China in the first part of this century, as it signaled the emergence of modern nationalism as a dominant force in Chinese politics. The student movement in Peking gained support from newspapers, intellectuals, political leaders, and peasants. The next 30 years of Chinese political life were largely caught up in a search for the most effective means of enacting the nationalist sentiments first expressed in 1919. China's abject weakness, as evidenced by its economic subjugation by foreigners, its inability to control the rise of the warlords, and its occupation by Japan, could ultimately find remedy only in nationally-derived strength and self-reliance.

An answer was given on October 1, 1949 as Mao Tse-tung (who had been an assistant librarian at Peking University during the May 4th Movement) stood on the rostrum of the Gate of Heavenly Peace facing Tien An Men Square. Standing literally before thousands of years of Chinese history, Mao proclaimed the founding of the People's Republic of China, declaring that "The Chinese People have stood up!"

1 Summer Palace
2 Peking University
3 Capital Gymnasium
4 Peking Zoo
5 Peking Planetarium
6 Min Dzu (Nationalities) Hotel
7 Hsi Tan Market
8 Cultural Palace for the National Minorities
9 Peking Telegraph Building
10 Pei Hai Park
11 Coal Hill (Ching Shan)
12 Imperial Palace (Forbidden City)
13 Tien An Men
14 Great Hall of the People
15 Tien An Men Square
16 Museums of History and Revolution
17 Mao Tse-tung Memorial Hall
18 South Gate (Chien Men)
19 Shopping Area for Antiques
20 Peking Department Store
21 Peking Hotel
22 Temple of Heaven
23 Capital Hospital
24 Hsin Chiao Hotel
25 US Liaison Office
26 Workers Stadium
27 Friendship Store

PEKING

TO GREAT WALL
TO MING TOMBS

CHANGPING RD.

PEIHUAN RD.

ANTINGMENWAI RD.

TUNGCHIHMEN RD.

TO AIRPORT

H YUAN LU

HSINCHIEHKOU RD.

HSICHIHMEN RD.

TUNGCHIH RD.

KUNGJEN TIYUCHANG RD.

TI AN MEN RD.

26

CHENGMEN RD.

10

11

WANGFUCHING RD.

TUNGSZU RD.

TUNGTACHIAO RD.

12

TUNGTAN RD.

HOPING RD.

CHIHTAN RD.

LISHIH RD.

HSITAN RD.

7

20

23

25

27

6   8   9

21

13

CHANGAN RD.

CHIENKUO RD.

TUNGHUAN RD.

14 15 16

17

24

18

PEKING
RAILROAD
STATION

LIU LI CHANG RD.

19

KUANGCHUMEN RD.

MEN RD.

CHIENMEN RD.

22

Map © 1978, Eurasia Press, Inc.

Economy and Culture

Since 1949, Peking's industrial development has been rapid and diverse. Although the city still ranks behind Shanghai and Shenyang as a manufacturing center, Peking has become a major producer of textiles and synthetic fibers, petrochemicals, automotive and agricultural equipment, and light and heavy machinery. Recent growth has emphasized manufacture of communications and electronics equipment, as well as advanced military weapons. Peking's factories also produce railroad cars, newsprint, and machine tools.

Expansion is itself an important industry in Peking. Since 1960, new construction has enlarged the original area by one-third, with over 150 major new residential complexes built since 1949. Large public works projects include the subway, a vast underground network of air-raid shelters, and monumental structures such as the Great Hall of the People, several national museums, and the Mao Tse-tung Memorial Hall. Major projects —and their maintenance— continue to employ large segments of the workforce. In 1978, a new airport was to open with a 3,200-m. (10,496-ft.) runway.

Peking's artisans are famous for their handicraft work. Carpets, embroidery, silks, ivory carving, paintings (both new styles and classical reproductions), jade, cloisonné, and lacquerware are of the highest quality. A museum has been established to display the best of these artisan skills.

The city's thousands of fruit and vegetable stands are nearly all supplied by the surrounding region, where some 275,000 acres are under cultivation. The area southwest of Peking is extremely fertile, and the creation of reservoirs and irrigation systems has assured a continuous food supply. There is an eight-month growing season in this part of China. Cereals grown include wheat, rice, maize, sorghum, barley, and kaoliang. Local vegetables are also important. These include cabbage, turnips, spinach, tomatoes, cucumbers, eggplant, sweet potatoes, beans, soybeans, peas, lotus root, onions, and garlic. There is also a wide variety of fruits—peaches, apricots, apples, pears, and persimmons (which can be seen drying on the slate roofs in the October sun). A variety of farm animals and poultry (Peking ducks!) are raised on neighboring communes.

There are many institutes of higher learning in Peking. Several help to support the capital's large and growing skilled labor force through excellent technical research facilities. The prestigious Peking and Tsing Hua universities are here, as are several language institutes, theater and drama companies, and the Institute for National

View of Tien An Men Square

Minorities (where minority representatives receive academic and political training prior to their return to leadership positions within their native groups). The cultural life of Peking is further enhanced by 25 theaters and numerous cinemas.

HIGHLIGHTS FOR TRAVELERS

☐ **Mao Tse-tung Memorial Hall.** Few men in world history have had the impact of Mao Tse-tung. His stature as an international figure and as the pre-eminent leader of the People's Republic of China is symbolized by the Chairman Mao Tse-tung Memorial Hall on the south end of Tien An Men Square. In the past, emperors chose their own monuments and built them away from the cities where they lived. Quite appropriately, perhaps, Mao Tse-tung has been interred in the heart of Peking, close to the masses he served until his death on September 8, 1976. The cornerstone for the Memorial Hall was laid by Mao's successor, Chairman Hua Kuo-feng, on November 24, 1976. It was completed on September 8, 1977, a year after Mao's death.

Located just south of the Monument to the People's Heroes and just north of Peking's South Gate, the Memorial Hall is a structure measuring 105 m. (344.4 ft.) square. The flat, low-tiered roof with its golden-yellow glazed tile cornices is supported by 44 granite pillars. In the north hall, facing Tien An Men, is a white marble statue of

Mao Tse-tung. Inside the mausoleum itself, Mao's remains recline in a crystal sarcophagus, the red flag of the Communist Party of China draped over his body.

In the southern hall is a huge marble scroll on which the following poem is engraved in Chairman Mao's handwriting:

Reply to Comrade Kuo Mo-jo—
to the tune of Man Chiang Hung

On this tiny globe
A few flies dash themselves against the wall,
Humming without cease,
Sometimes shrilling,
Sometimes moaning.
Ants on the locust tree assume a great nation swagger
And mayflies lightly plot to topple the giant tree.
The west wind scatters leaves over Changan,
And the arrows are flying, twanging.

So many deeds cry out to be done,
And always urgently;
The world rolls on,
Time presses.
Ten thousand years are too long,
Seize the day, seize the hour!
The Four Seas are rising, clouds and waters raging,
The Five Continents are rocking, wind and thunder roaring.
Our force is irresistible,
Away with all pests!
January 9, 1963

Tien An Men

This name is applied generally to the central square of Peking, and encompasses Tien An Men Gate, Tien An Men Square, and several important monuments and buildings. Just as the Imperial Palace represents the "closed in" trappings of the past, Tien An Men today explicitly declares China's "open" future.

☐ **Gate of Heavenly Peace (Tien An Men).** This massive stone gate with its wooden roof was built in 1412 and restored in 1651. A stream flows at the foot of the gate, spanned by five sculptured white marble bridges. A central portal is dominated by an immense portrait of Mao Tse-tung. On top is a rostrum where, on special occasions, China's leaders present themselves to the people. Inscribed on each side of the portal are two durable political slogans: on the left, "Long Life to the People's Republic of China!;" on the right, "Long Live the Unity of the Peoples of the World!" The grandstands below have a capacity of 20,000, usually filled by official guests reviewing parades and partaking in celebrations.

□ **Tien An Men Square.** Tien An Men Gate overlooks the largest public square in the world. Originally covering 27 acres, the site was rebuilt in 1958 (during a massive, city-wide face-lifting campaign) and extended to 98 acres. Each flagstone is numbered so that parade units can line up in the appropriate sequence.

□ **Monument to the People's Heroes.** In the center of the square is an obelisk 36 m. (118 ft.) high, a tribute to the heroes who died in the cause of the revolution. The cornerstone was laid by Chairman Mao and the structure completed on May 1, 1958. A bas-relief of soldiers, peasants, and workers depicts key episodes in the revolution (the sequence begins from the east side). The obelisk carries two inscriptions. One, in Chairman Mao's calligraphy, states "The People's Heroes Are Immortal." A second, longer text, by Chou En-lai, is one of the rare public examples of his calligraphy.

□ **South Gate (Chien Men).** The Gate, recently refurbished to better complement the Mao Tse-tung Memorial Hall, was originally built in the 15th century. It once connected the north and south towns, but recently the surrounding area has been cleared so as to accommodate the subway and the widened east-west street to the south.

□ **Great Hall of the People.** On the eastern side of the square is the Great Hall of the People, referred to in some older guides as the National People's Congress Building.

This great hall, built over a course of just ten months during 1958-59, can accommodate a meeting of 10,000 delegates. On the occasion of Richard Nixon's visit to China in 1972, it held 5,000 dinner guests. There are also a number of reception rooms of various sizes where top-ranking leaders conduct interviews with foreigners. The building occupies 51,520 sq. m. (61,600 sq. yd.) and extends 310 m. (1,017 ft.) from north to south.

□ **Museum of the Revolution and Museum of History.** Two large buildings dominate the eastern side of Tien An Men Square. These are the Museum of History (covering periods up to 1840) and the

Museum of the Revolution (after 1840). The former has been closed since the Cultural Revolution; the Museum of the Revolution has recently reopened with a display on the life of Chou En-lai.

☐ **Cultural Palace of the Minorities.** Less than a mile and a half west of Tien An Men stands a large rectangular structure with a 13-story (195-ft.) tower. This is the Cultural Palace of the Minorities, dedicated to the cultural contributions of China's minority peoples. The building is a gay array of yellow stucco with green trim and a turquoise tile roof, giving the impression of a traditional Chinese design draped over a Western frame. Completed in 1959, it has four sections: a cultural center, theater, library, and a museum with 18 exhibition halls.

China's national minorities are credited with important status by the PRC government. While the Han (Chinese) people make up 94% of China's population, the remaining 6% inhabit nearly 60% of China's territory, giving them political significance well beyond their numbers.

Great Hall of the People

The Imperial Palace (Ku Kung)

Also known as the "Forbidden City" and the "Palace Museum," this complex is both a mecca for tourists and an abiding symbol of traditional China. The entire complex has over 9,000 rooms and comprises the largest and most complete group of ancient buildings that has survived to the present age. Although it is old China's most imposing complex, its simple architectural lines play down its grand scale and lend a feeling of peaceful, harmonious solidity.

The Palace was built largely during the period 1406-20, under the reign of the Ming Emperor Yung Lo and was inhabited by each of the remaining 12 Ming emperors. Sacked and looted by the Manchus during the Ming Dynasty's overthrow, the complex was restored to its original splendor under later Ch'ing rulers (mainly by Emperor Ch'ien Lung, 1736-96). It acquired its "Forbidden" name because entry by common citizens (and foreigners) was regarded as a capital offense. Under the People's Republic of China, the area has been converted into a public museum, open to all.

Nearly all of the buildings are two stories high, flanked by courtyards whose proportions vary with the importance of the palaces to which they were attached. Overall, the Imperial Palace covers an area of 250 acres, and is surrounded by a moat and a 35-ft. wall with towers on each corner.

The palace grounds are divided into two sections. The foregrounds consist of three large public halls from which the Ming and Ch'ing emperors issued edicts and decrees and conducted important state ceremonies. The rear part of the complex is made up of three main palaces, a few smaller "east" and "west" palaces, and the Imperial Gardens. In this setting, emperors divided their time between the affairs of state and their families.

The Palace Foregrounds

☐ **Meridian Gate (Wu Men).** Wu Men demarcates the main entrance to the Forbidden City. It was first built in 1420 and restored in 1647. It was here that the emperor presided over military ceremonies and announced each year's new calendar (even the months and days were the province of the emperor). The imposing doors are festooned with wooden carvings and a set of lion-head knockers.

☐ **Hall of Supreme Harmony (T'ai Ho Tien).** The Meridian Gate opens onto a large paved courtyard traversed by a small river. Opposite, the courtyard is guarded by a smaller gate, the T'ai Ho Men (Hall of Supreme Harmony Gate), fronted by two stylized bronze lions.

The Hall, built in 1420 and restored in 1697 during Emperor K'ang Hsi's reign, is 35 m. (115 ft.) high, and has an area of 2,377 sq. m. (2,843 sq.yd.). It is the tallest and most expansive of the palace buildings, and was used by the emperor on special occasions. The emperor's original throne is preserved here, surrounded by screens, four cloisonné incense burners, and a setting of ornate furniture.

In its more current history, the courtyard was the scene of a ceremony held by Western and Chinese military troops to celebrate the end of World War I.

☐ **Hall of Perfect Harmony (Chung Ho Tien).** Passing through the Hall of Supreme Harmony, one descends 28 steps into the largest courtyard of the Palace, beyond which is the Hall of Perfect Harmony. The hall was built in 1420, restored in 1627, and further renovated in 1690. Used by the emperor to don formal regalia before entering the Hall of Supreme Harmony, it was also where he performed such ceremonies as examining seeds for the new planting.

☐ **Hall of Preserving Harmony (Pao Ho Tien).** This Hall was built in 1420, rebuilt in 1625, and repaired in 1765. In 1789, it became the site of the "Palace Examinations," the highest stage of the Imperial Examination System and ostensibly the origin of all modern meritocracies. Successful candidates won the title of Chin Shih (loosely, "scholars"). Graduates of the system passed into high positions in government and administration throughout the empire, and their future wealth and status was assured. Although frequently undermined by corruption, the system did provide a modicum of upward mobility in traditional Chinese society.

The original throne remains in this room, and is surrounded by some fine bronzes. The Hall's anterooms have been converted to museum galleries that display relics of the imperial households.

The flight of steps behind this Hall is called the "dragon pavement." The largest stone carving in the Imperial Palace, it is a work of the Ming period.

Rear Section of the Palace Grounds

☐ **Palace of Heavenly Purity (Ch'ien Ch'ing Kung).** Entering the courtyard of this hall, the visitor passes through the Gate of Heavenly Purity, the longest-standing original structure in the compound. (The

Palace of Heavenly Purity itself was burned and restored three times since its original construction in 1420.)

From the Ming to the early Ch'ing Dynasty, emperors resided and handled routine affairs of state in these quarters. The terrace surrounding the palace has gilt incense burners, bronze tortoises and cranes, a sundial, and a few miniature temples. The palace was last used for an "imperial" occasion in 1922 when the former child emperor, P'u Yi, last of the Ch'ing Dynasty imperial line, was married. Following the demise of the empire in 1911, P'u Yi (who carried the name "Henry") was employed as a gardener on the palace grounds.

☐ **Hall of Union (Chiao T'ai Tien).** Used by the Ch'ing emperors for birthday celebrations, this hall was built in 1420 and rebuilt in 1655. On display is one of ancient China's most remarkable scientific inventions, a clepsydra (water clock)—a mechanism that dates back 2,500 years. On the west side of the hall is a mechanical clock made by the Works Department of the Imperial Board in 1797.

☐ **Palace of Earthly Tranquility (K'un Ning Kung).** The Ming empress lived in this palace which was built in 1420. Later, Ch'ing rulers used it as a place to offer sacrifices. An eastern side-room was used as a bridal chamber.

Tien T'ang, Temple of Heaven

□ **East and West Palaces.** To the sides of these main halls are a series of six eastern and six western palaces used for libraries, ceremonies, living quarters, and so on. Today, they house exhibitions that include furniture, jewelry, and other household items. Usually, only one or two rooms are opened for inspection.

□ **Imperial Gardens.** At the rear of the Palaces are the Imperial Gardens, which cover 7,000 sq. m. (8,400 sq. yd.) and were originally built during the Ming Dynasty. The pines and cypresses growing here are several hundred years old. The grounds are arrayed with statues, rock gardens, pebble walkways laid out in intricate designs, and an artificial mountain (built in 1538) adorned with a cave, waterfall, and pavilion.

A visit to the Imperial Palace usually consumes a full morning or afternoon. Visitors leave through the rear gate (Cheng Kuang Men), a simple portal guarded by two gilded bronze elephants. The grounds are exited through the massive Gate of Divine Pride (Shen Wu Men), where buses wait for the return trip to the hotel.

Areas Surrounding the Imperial Palace

Within the compound and on its flanks are some worthwhile sites not normally included in tours.

□ **The Chinese History Museum.** A museum complex on the eastern side of the Ku Kung features a special archeological exhibition that traces the gamut of Chinese history. It can be reached by walking east on the road that runs between Wu Men and T'ai Ho T'ien. The collection includes a remarkable jade burial garment and an assortment of carved stone horses and warriors unearthed in 1976 near Sian. Advance permission must be obtained for visits to this musuem.

□ **Sun Yat-sen Park.** Just inside the Tien An Men Gate, there are two large public gardens. On the west is Sun Yat-sen Park, situated on a site laid out in 1421. It affords a convenient place to relax from the rigors of sightseeing, and to walk slowly among the trees, sip tea, and watch Peking's citizens at their leisure.

□ **People's Cultural Park.** The People's Park may be found by turning east after entering the Tien An Men Gate. With a tree-lined boulevard in the shadow of the old imperial walls, this is a popular place for morning exercise, music practice, badminton, or just a leisurely stroll along the moat.

□ **Coal Hill (Mei Shan or Ching Shan).** Coal Hill is situated directly opposite the exit gate of the Imperial Gardens. Now more com-

Coal Hill

monly called Ching Shan (Prospect Hill), it was used by the emperors to bring a little of the countryside into the flat plain of Peking. They stocked the area with hares and other small game.

Closed for "renovations" during the Cultural Revolution, it was reopened to the public in March 1978. Sites in the park include the Beautiful View Tower (Chi Wang Lou) and the Pavilion of Everlasting Springs (Wan Chun Ting), which commands a breathtaking view of the Imperial Palace and the full expanse of the capital.

□ **Chung Nan Hai.** This is the combined name for "middle and southern lake," which flanks the Imperial Palace to the west. As it is the area where China's present leaders live and work, it is closed off to visitors. The entrance to this compound is about a half-mile east from the center of Tien An Men. A flag pole and soldiers standing guard mark the gate.

□ **Pei Hai (North Lake).** Closed for "renovations" until March 1978 (as a result of the Cultural Revolution), this park is one of the loveliest in Peking. It was originally built about 300 AD and is a favorite spot for the local population. Its beauty is subtle and can best be appreciated on a weekday when it tends to be less crowded. There is a pagoda, built in 1650, and a round tower that dates from 1740. The Bridge of Perfect Wisdom (Chih Chu Ch'iao) is one of the park's more famous landmarks.

☐ **The Great Wall.** Rising and falling with the ridges of the northern hills and undulating far off into the distance, the Great Wall consistently exceeds the expectations of visitors. The only man-made object visible from earth orbit, the wall remains one of the most astonishing feats of human endeavor. The amount of brick and stone employed to construct the Great Wall could be used to surround the earth with a dike eight feet high.

Once, the Great Wall stretched from the Po Hai Sea in the east to the Chiayukuan in Kansu Province to the west, winding its way over a length of 10,000 ancient Chinese *li* (about 5,000 km. or 3,100 mi.). Construction began during the Warring States (480-422 BC) period, when different sections were built in scattered areas.

Following China's unification under the first Ch'in Emperor (221-207 BC), 300,000 men (many of them political prisoners) were put to work connecting the segments into one huge rampart of stone and earth. From the end of the 16th century AD until the Ming Dynasty, the Great Wall was frequently overrun and became obsolete as an effective barrier against determined invaders (for whom bribes became the most effective weapons). The Ming emperors, successors to the Mongols, again tried to make it into a useful fortification, adding cement, bricks, and blocks of stone. The wall was made wide enough to accommodate six horses running abreast. Overall, it averages 6.6 m. (22 ft.) in height and 5.8 m. (19 ft.) in width. Battlements, built at intervals of 140 m. (459 ft.), were used as signal towers.

A two-hour bus (or train) ride to the north of Peking passes agricultural communes, market towns, extensive rock quarries, and, finally, leads into the rugged, rock-strewn foothills that once formed China's northern frontier. Here, at Pataling Pass, a section of the wall has been restored, and one can climb either left or right—for 500 yards or so—to the top of the closest hill.

☐ **The Ming Tombs.** In keeping with an imperial tradition that dated back to the Chou Dynasty, the Ming emperors selected the location and design of their tombs while they were still alive. Construction of the tomb site began in 1584 and was completed in four years at a cost of 4 million oz. of silver. All but one Ming emperor (T'ai Tzu, buried in Nanking) chose to be buried in this beautiful valley 48 km. (30 mi.) north of Peking.

The road to the tombs, which branches off from the route to the Great Wall, was once a four-mile-long sacred way, forbidden to all but the emperor's retinue. Today, the bus first drives through a great marble gate (built in 1540) with five arches. About a mile further up the road is the Great Red Gate (Ta Hung Men), a massive 36.6 m. (120 ft.) portal on which were formerly hung three huge wooden doors. Just beyond the gate sits a stone tortoise with a stele inscribed by the fourth Ming emperor (1426). Thirty feet high, it is the largest stone tablet of this type in China. Here begins the famous "Avenue of the Animals" (tours will stop here after a visit to the Tomb itself, but only if time allows). Lions, camels, elephants, horses, and two sets of mythical beasts, totaling 12 statues, line each side of the road, alternately standing and kneeling. Following are a series of stone statues of 12 imperial ministers, all dating from the 15th century.

Of the tombs themselves, only two have been excavated, those of Chang Ling and Ting Ling. The sepulchre of the first has not been opened, however. Visitors are taken to the tomb of Ting Ling, who was buried here with two wives in 1620 in a marble vault some four stories underground. The entrance to the grounds is marked by a large gate with a magnificent bronze lion. Through the gate several museum buildings house tomb objects. Thereafter, the walkway leads up the hill to the tomb itself.

Gate of Summer Palace

☐ **Summer Palace.** The Summer Palace lies seven miles northwest of Peking, and is a favorite of Peking residents for a cool, breezy picnic in summer, and for skating on Kunming Lake in winter.

There have actually been two Summer Palaces. The original was built by the Jurchen Tartars during the Chin Kingdom (1115-1234 AD) where Peking University now stands, and maintained until the

Marble Barge

late Ch'ing Dynasty when, in 1860, the British burned it in an effort to compel the imperial court to "see reason."

The present Summer Palace is largely the work of the Ch'ing emperors, and is set on 283 hectares (700 acres) of land on the shores of Kunming Lake. The Emperor Ch'ien Lung built the Pai Yun (White Cloud) Palace on top of Longevity Hill in 1791 as a tribute to his 60-year-old mother. The Empress Tsu Hsi extended the palaces and the lovely "Painted Gallery," a wooden walkway 728 m. (2,388 ft.) long that girds the north shore of the lake. Its wooden beams are painted with exquisite landscapes. Tsu Hsi is also responsible for the Marble Boat, built by funds diverted from their intended use in creating China's first modern navy.

A complete tour of the Summer Palace requires a full day. Unfortunately, most visits are alloted only half that time. The best view is provided from the top of Longevity Hill, which affords a panorama of the lake, with its traditional humpbacked (17-arched) bridges, the exotic Jade Belt Bridge, a lovely pagoda, and the Garden of Harmonious Interests (Hsieh Ch'ou Yuan). Shimmering in the summer sun, the glazed golden tiles of the palaces impart the feeling of a traditional Chinese landscape painting.

☐ **Temple of Heaven.** The Temple of Heaven is one of traditional China's most striking monuments. Its 15th-century planners used the most advanced principles of architecture, mechanics, and geometry known at the time. The aesthetic goal was to create a structure that blended harmoniously with sky and earth.

The temple and its accompanying buildings are set in a large park (6.1 sq. km.—2.4 sq. mi.) to the south of Peking. The grounds are expansive enough so that the everyday sounds of Peking do not intrude. Indeed, silence adds to the aura.

The Temple of Heaven was built in 1420. It was first restored in 1751 and, after a fire begun by lightning, rebuilt in 1889. After 1949, scientists carefully studied the paint pigments and wooden structure so as to recreate precisely its original splendor. The temple had been used by emperors as a personal altar to pray for better harvests and to seek heaven's blessing on events of the coming year.

The building is set on a triple-tiered round marble terrace, each layer surrounded by a balustrade 11 m. (36 ft.) high. The base of the temple is 96 ft. in diameter, and is topped by a triple cone-shaped roof of blue-glazed tiles (representing the sky), culminating in a gilded ball. Not a single nail was used in the construction. The interlaced wooden frame is supported by 28 columns hewn from trees brought from Yunnan. There are four large support pillars in the interior, each 18.3 m. (60 ft.) high. The roof is supported on an articulated skeleton, without the use of ceiling joists.

Nearby, in the courtyard of the main temple, are two auxiliary buildings. Their cone-shaped roofs are miniature versions of the main temple. The point of interest here is the "Echo Wall." Two people standing on opposite sides of the courtyard near the wall can hear each other's speech without raising their voices. Moreover, three large stones that lie in the central walkway leading to the main temple, known as the "Three Echoing Stones," display further acoustic oddities. A single shout or hand-clap from the first stone produces a single echo; a double echo is produced on the second stone; and on the third, three echoes. (The effect is due to the different distances of the stones from the walls, producing measured variations in the distance for sound reflection.)

The southern part of the complex has the equally fascinating Round Mound, consisting of three round white marble terraces first built in 1539 and enlarged in 1749. When standing on the center stone, a voice will appear to come back louder and fuller than the original spoken word, giving the effect of an echo chamber. (Sound waves are amplified by reverberating across the round walls and stone fences before being reflected back.)

Of final note are the numerological patterns built into the architectural features of the Temple of Heaven complex. The main temple has 28 pillars: the four main pillars holding up the temple represent the four seasons, and the 12 interior posts the months of the year. In ancient days, the Chinese divided the day into 12-hour periods, represented by the outer ring of 12 pillars. The symbolic number nine, signifying the sky (or heaven) and the emperor, recurs in the design of the Round Mound. Thus, the flagstones on the upper terrace are arranged in concentric circles in multiples of nine; i.e., the first circle has 9 stones, the second 18, and so on to a final total of 243 in the 27th and outermost ring.

☐ **Marco Polo Bridge (Lu Kuo Chiao).** Although not a stop on most itineraries, the bridge is usually crossed when traveling to the western and southern suburbs (en route to Peking Petrochemical Factory, for example). The bridge lies about 16 km. (10 mi.) southwest of the city, spanning the Yungting River. The Chinese name for the bridge is Lu Kuo Chiao (Reedy Moat Bridge), and it dates back some 780 years. Marco Polo visited the area in 1190, later describing the bridge in expansive terms, and thus giving it its nickname.

The original bridge was washed away by a flood in 1698, but a faithful replica was built in its place. It is constructed of white marble and is 235 m. (770 ft.) long, supported by 11 arches. It was widened in 1969, but the original balustrades, containing some 280 parapets adorned with miniature stone lions, were retained.

The bridge is famous as the site of the "Marco Polo Incident," a 1937 clash between Chinese and Japanese troops that helped spark the anti-Japanese war.

☐ **Peking Zoo.** If seen at all, the zoo is usually tacked onto visitors' itineraries as part of a long day of sightseeing. This practice is unfortunate, since the zoo is worth more than the standard, cursory visit to its most famous inhabitants, the pandas.

The Peking Zoo dates from the Ming Dynasty when it was the site of an imperial park. A zoological garden was established on the site during the Ch'ing Dynasty, but only a dozen or so animals had survived by 1949. Much expansion has gone on since, and now the Peking Zoo boasts more than 2,000 animals of 300 species. Some of the more prized species are the giraffes, lions, polar bears, roe deer, and gibbon apes. One of the two musk oxen given to China by President Nixon (in exchange for the two pandas now in Washington) is still alive. The best known panda variety is the giant panda, native to China. A smaller, brown species is more directly related to the racoon, and suffers in the shadow of its more glamorous cousin.

The large domed building across the street is the Peking Planetarium.

☐ **Peking Petrochemical Plant.** Peking has more of interest than its historical monuments, and a visit to China's capital is likely to include at least one tour of a modern factory or other industrial site. China is justly proud of its petroleum industry, and visitors are sometimes taken to the Peking Petrochemical Plant, about a two-hour drive past the Marco Polo Bridge. The complex is Chinese in design and execution (although some Romanian technical equipment has been added). It consists of ten major plants. It has an annual capacity of 7 million tons and processes 50 varieties of fuels and lubricants. It also makes synthetic fibers and rubber products. Some of the crude oil comes from the famous Taching Oil Field near Harbin, some 1,600 km. (994 mi.) to the north.

Management personnel told visitors that 1977 saw a 42% increase in oil-processing capacity, and that the state target was fulfilled by December 26 (Mao's birthday). There were some 30,000 workers in 1978 (35% women), but the complex is being expanded to employ 100,000. The average wage is Y60 per month (US$35.30). Capital investment has totaled over Y4 billion (US$2.35 billion). The plant has its own schools (including six high schools), nurseries, a hospital, and a large expanse of modern workers' housing.

☐ **Peking University.** Since Peking is also a center of education, tours are likely to include one of the city's famous universities. Peking University was founded in 1898 as Yenching University, a US-sponsored institution. Many of its students partook in the May 4th Movement of 1919. And it was here that the debates giving rise to the Cultural Revolution (1966-68) began. During that period, many of its most noted professors, under attack by the Red Guards, publicly confessed their guilt for putting academic pursuits ahead of revolutionary ideals. By 1977, however, most were restored to their former posts and the promotion of research and academic achievement was receiving support from the highest echelons of China's new leadership. In 1978, its 3,000 students were augmented by several thousand more who, in the fall of 1977, took the first nationwide university-entrance examinations held in China since 1966.

WALKING TOURS

There is no better place in China for a walk than Peking. The symmetry of the city's layout facilitates wandering through the varied matrix of dusty alleyways and broad boulevards. (Since city streets in China tend to change names every several blocks, a good map should be brought along for back-up.) Because Peking is so spread out, walkers should not expect to "do the town" in one afternoon or even in one day. It is better advised to set out in a taxi to a particular area of town (e.g., the Temple of Heaven) and then walk back, saving valuable time and energy.

The best period for walking is in the early morning, as near to sunrise as one can manage. In the early morning light, the sun glistens on the yellow roofs of the Palace Museum. Mornings are times for recreation in China and outside its red ochre walls can be heard the strains of the flute or violin, a Peking Opera aria, the recitation of a poem, or the blare of a bugle. Individuals or groups fill the open spaces to practice *t'ai ch'i ch'uan* ("shadow boxing") and *wu shu* (traditional martial arts) or to play badminton, basketball, or other sports.

But the main thing is to take to the streets and look at the people of Peking—their neighborhoods, their stores, their places of work, and the quiet, earnest industry that marks all aspects of their lives.

The two suggested walking tours that follow begin at the Peking Hotel.

☐ **A Market Walk: Wang Fu Ching** (30 minutes or more—round trip distance, 2.2 mi.)

Although Wang Fu Ching is best known as the busiest shopping district in Peking, it is also one of Peking's more venerable neighborhoods. Wang Fu Ching is the street immediately to the east of the Peking Hotel. To reach it, one should proceed north. Three blocks to the right down San T'iao Hu Tung is the Capital Hospital, a pre-1949 structure built with grants from the Rockefeller Foundation. On the next block (Shuai Fu Yuan) is the China Art Gallery, followed by the Tung Feng people's market. This is the crossroads of Tung An Men and at this point shops begin to thin out. Two and a half blocks further is the Eastern Church. Three blocks further is the Capital Theater, and two blocks beyond that, on the left, is the Academia Sinica Institute of History and its library.

The main hotel for overseas Chinese is on the corner of the next major intersection of Han Hua Yuan Ta Chieh, to the left, and Chu Shih Ta Chieh, to the right. The Museum of Fine Arts, on the northwest corner, often carries exhibitions of both foreign and Chinese art.

☐ **A Sunrise Walk: Tien An Men** (1 hour, 4.2 km—2.6 mi.)

This excursion is designed to let the visitor observe morning exercises and commuting activity in Peking. The walk begins by turning right out the main door of the Peking Hotel and following Chang An Boulevard toward Tien An Men. Enter the Tien An Men Gate and walk north towards the Wu Men Gate of the main Imperial Palace. To the left there will be an entrance to Sun Yat-sen Park; to the right, the Working People's Park. Either is worth walking through.

Or, one can procede straight on, turning right (east) just before Wu Men, passing through a relatively small gate and following the road along the wall. The area astride the moat is a favorite for Wushu artists and badminton players. Continuing along the wall as the road turns left, head east again at the first chance—across a large bridge that spans the moat (the only one in the vicinity). The walker has now reached Tung An Men Ta Chieh. This should be followed past two large intersections, until it crosses Wang Fu Ching. The Peking Hotel (and breakfast) are four short blocks away on the right.

HOTEL ACCOMMODATIONS

☐ **Peking Hotel.** Completed in 1975, the Peking Hotel is among the country's most modern, and boasts architectural and service features found in no other PRC hotels. Its location is excellent: around the corner is Wang Fu Ching, Peking's main shopping district. Tien An Men is two long blocks away.

The hotel consists of three wings. The western wing was built in the early 1950s in grand Soviet style, with an ornate lobby and wood-paneled rooms. Now rarely used by foreigners, it is retained for high-ranking PRC officials and citizens. The middle wing is used as a service area, with dormitories for workers and large rooms for film-showings and meetings.

The new wing—by far the tallest building in Peking—is used exclusively by foreign guests. It has 141,000 sq. m. (168,636 sq. yd.) of floor space spread over 17 stories (with no 13th floor). Eight elevators serve 900 rooms with 1,800 beds. There is a large (almost cavernous) waiting room with a refreshment bar and retail shop, a red-carpeted lobby (with a map of the world displaying times around the globe), a billiards room, post and telegraph office (open 8 AM-6:30 PM), a bank (8-11 AM; 2-5 PM), chess rooms, and a bookshop. The central building in the old wing has a grocery store. A barbershop and hairdresser is located on the second floor.

The kitchen serves Szechwan, Cantonese, Huaiyang, Tanchie, and Western dishes. The dining room is open from 7:00-8:30 AM for breakfast; noon-2:00 PM for lunch; and 6:00-8:30 PM for dinner. Although both food and service have sharply deteriorated in recent years, a rotation of service workers in 1977 was expected to improve the situation.

Delegations and tour groups are assigned tables, usually towards the back of the room beneath a huge mosaic of scenes from Kweilin. Businessmen usually occupy the front tables, often engaging in "tourist watching" to help relieve long weeks of negotiations. The touches of home found on different tables—instant coffee, jams, honey—usually belong to these "regulars."

Rooms are comfortable, clean, and good-sized, and feature drapes that are electrically controlled. Balconies on some rooms offer a spectacular view of Peking, particularly those that look west over the Forbidden City and the hills beyond. The service desks provide laundry and dry-cleaning services, and sell refreshments (including beer, wine, and soda), cigarettes, and other sundries. The hotel staff is available to polish shoes and carry out minor repairs.

The Peking Hotel is located on Chang An Chieh (telephone: 55831). Its rates per night are Y55 (US$32.35) for a twin room, and Y155 (US$67.65) for a suite including a refrigerator and radio.

□ **Hsin Chiao (New Citizen) Hotel.** This six-story hotel, built in the Soviet style and located to the southeast of Tien An Men in the old legation quarter, used to be an exclusive haunt for foreign journalists, businessmen, and other "new China hands." The new wing of the Peking Hotel (where the prices are suitably higher) has taken away some of the Hsin Chiao's clientele, although there remains a warm familiarity about the place.

Rooms are just large enough to accommodate twin beds, a desk, and two easy chairs. There is a Chinese dining room on the lobby floor, but most guests prefer the Western dining room on the sixth floor, which provides a lovely view of the city. For some foreigners, the hotel's main attraction is a bar (until the opening of the Peking Hotel, the only one in town) and a roof garden that stays open late into the evenings during the warm summer months. The usual range of services is available.

The Hsin Chiao (New Citizen) Hotel is located on Tsung Wen Men (telephone: 557731). Its rates per night are Y9 (US$5.30) without bath, and Y14 (US$8.24) with bath.

☐ **Min Dzu (Nationalities) Hotel.** The 11-story Min Dzu is in most ways the most old-fashioned and basic of the hotels reserved for foreign guests in Peking. Nevertheless, it is clean, has a góod dining room, and provides excellent services.

The hotel is located almost two miles due west along Chang An Boulevard from Tien An Men, and is thus not convenient to Peking's central sites. Nearby, however, is the Hsi-tan market area, a colorful district almost as well-stocked as Wang Fu Ching across town.

Rooms are plain, with brown coverlets adorning straw-mattressed beds. There are the customary two chairs, dresser, and desk. As in most other hotels, bathrooms are old-fashioned (e.g., hand-showers) but adequate. They are supplied with soap, towels, and—surprisingly—combs. A thermos with hot water is provided for making tea (also supplied in little wooden boxes) and there is a carafe filled with drinking water.

The Min Dzu is located on Chang An Boulevard (telephone: 668541). Its rates per night are Y17 (US$10) for a single twin-bedded room and Y34 (US$20) for a double room.

PEKING'S CUISINE

Of course, there is Peking Duck. But there are also a wide range of other specialities to try. Peking cuisine is really a mixture of many styles from northern China, including Mongolian, Shantung, and even Szechwan. Highly recommended dishes include hot-and-sour soup (with emphasis usually on the hot), the cold preliminary dishes, dumplings, fried prawns, and sea slugs. A memorable dessert is apples covered with molten toffee (and then solidified in ice water).

All of this can be washed down with some excellent local beers: Peking or Tsingtao brands. There are some good local wines (made from kaoliang grains); the most highly regarded is the slightly sweet Shaohsing, usually warmed before serving.

☐ **Peiching Kaoya Tien (Peking Duck Restaurant).** Two branches of Peiching Kaoya Tien specialize in this justifiably famous local delicacy. The first one listed suffers the indignity of being referred to as the "sick duck"—because of its proximity to the Capital Hospital. It is located on a little lane found on the east side of Wang Fu Ching between numbers 170 and 180 (telephone: 553310). The other "duck" is located near the South Gate and Chien Men Street (751379). Reservations for both are advised since they are often crowded with banquet parties. Diners should be prepared for the expense—at least Y15 per person (mid-1977)—to get so much as a glimpse of the duck. A full duck dinner, including literally every part but its quack, is three times that amount.

☐ **Min Tsu Fan Chuang.** Peking has a host of minority-nationality restaurants, including several that feature hearty Mongolian cuisine. The Min Tsu offers the advantage of being close to the Peking Hotel. It is off Wang Fu Ching, at the north entrance of the East Wind market. From the hotel, go up Wang Fu Ching, turn right at the traffic light into Tung Hua Men, and follow a long block up the street to No. 160 (telephone: 550069). The dining section for foreigners is upstairs. Other recommended minority-nationality restaurants are the Hung Pin Lo (Hopei, Muslim) and the Sinkiang Tsan Ting.

☐ **Feng Tse Yuan.** Expensive, but worth it, since the Feng Tse is one of the famous restaurants of long standing in Peking. Given the proper budget and imagination, diners will be treated to a masterful, subtle meal. Feng Tse Yuan is located at 83 Zhu Shi Kou (telephone: 332828).

☐ **Cheng Tu.** A notable restaurant for its feisty Szechwan food (i.e., hot and spicy) and colorful atmosphere; several single-floor buildings are linked by cobblestone courtyards in the style of traditional China (telephone: 336356).

Those who crave a hot dog will find a reasonable facsimile at the Jitan Park Restaurant (open to foreigners only), which also serves good dumplings, the everyday dish of Peking.

SHOPPING

In addition to Peking's Friendship Store there are five main shopping areas: Wang Fu Ching and Liu Li Ch'ang—the two largest, and Sung Tang, Hsi Tan, and Chien Men. For those who have more time, fruitful bargain-hunting can be conducted at second-hand furniture shops.

☐ **Friendship Store.** Peking's is the largest Friendship Store in China; three floors are well-stocked with everything from jade jewelry to a wide variety of wines and spirits. It has a complete range of local goods, Chinese export products, and handicrafts. Even if Peking is the first stop in China, it may be wise to indulge shopping impulses here since many items may not be available anywhere else. It is also the only place in Peking (and for that matter, in all of China) that will provide packaging, customs clearance, and shipping of items—including those purchased elsewhere in Peking. There are no bargains in shipping charges, however, which may run as high as Y300 (US$176.50) per cu.m. (35 cu. ft.).

The Friendship Store is open from 9AM to 9PM daily; its Bank of China branch is open 9AM to 7PM to exchange money.

Wang Fu Ching

Peking's major general shopping area is Wang Fu Ching, a street adjoining the Peking Hotel. Turn left out of the hotel driveway and left again up the flagstone pavement.

The following shops are found on the west (left) side of Wang Fu Ching, heading north:

Street Number	Specialty
299	**Film shop.** Chinese and (sometimes) foreign films, photographic supplies, albums, and so on. Most Chinese color film is not of the same standard as Western varieties, although the quality of black-and-white film (Seagull brand) is good.
295	**Hi-fi shop.** A good way to see what Chinese record players, radios, and televisions look like. Prices are relatively high for larger equipment, which is rarely purchased by individuals in China.
265	**Jewelry shop.** In addition to selling jewelry on display (gold, silver, ivory, jade), this store will also set stones.
261	**Chop (signature seal) shop.** Outside of Liu Li Chang, this chop store offers the best variety. A small but well-chosen collection, especially in the lower price ranges.
255	**Pai Hou Ta Lou.** The large, five-story building, set back from the street, is Peking's biggest department store. Everyone from chauffeured army commanders to out-of-town Chinese shop here. A good selection of most common items, including sundries, tools, and housewares.
235	**Foreign Language Bookstore.** Probably the best selection of Chinese books in English (and other languages) in China. Interesting items include opera libretti, tourist maps of Peking, and postcards from all over the country.

Having now arrived at the first major intersection (marked by a traffic light), turn left. On the left-hand (south) side of the street are:

16	**Record shop.**
28	**China Stamp Export Company.** As the name indicates, a large selection of Chinese stamps are available, many arranged

in bound sets. Chinese stamps make colorful, informative souvenirs, even for non-collectors.

Returning back down Wang Fu Ching, and across the intersection, are the following shops (walking south):

142 **Tea shop.** A large variety of good teas.

156 **Shoe and hat store.** Includes a wide selection of inexpensive fur garments, including hats for both children and adults.

Next to 156, set in from the other store fronts and directly across from the department store is a "covered market" called the East Wind Market (just follow the crowds). A popular place for everything from clocks to ice cream, it combines many shops and stalls grouped together under one roof.

172 **Children's store.** Includes clothing, shoes, and toys.

174 **Clock shop.** Peking's largest collection of clocks and watches.

192 **Fur and leather shop.** Fur, suede (an especially good purchase in China), gloves, hats; most items can be made to order, although this may require too much time for most visitors.

200 **Peking Handicrafts Exhibition Center.** Two floors display a full range of handicrafts and supplies, from cloisonné to brushes and ink.

210 **Odd-hour bookstore.** Caters to those who have to work during the day. It is open only from 9 to 9:30 AM and from 7:30 to 9:30 PM, and hence earns the name "Early-Late Bookstore."

214 **New China Book Store.** The largest in Peking, carrying a large collection of literature and technical and scientific books, as well as posters on the second floor.

Liu Li Ch'ang

This narrow street, synonymous with antiques, is located in the heart of the old city of Peking, about a mile southwest of the Gate of Heavenly Peace. It is a cross street of Hsin Hua Road South, set in the middle of small lanes, old housing compounds (*hu-tungs*), and a bustling residential district.

Tour buses or taxis park directly in front of the bookstore on the northeast corner of Liu Li Chang and Hsin Hua roads. The following shops align the east side of Liu Li Ch'ang:

136 **Rubbing and Figurine Shop.** Directly across the parking lot from the bookstore, this shop carries inexpensive Han funerary-tile rubbings, both black and white and in color (US $.60-5.00), as well as reproductions of Han and T'ang Dynasty funerary figures such as ceramic horses and figurines. (Some items now fall in the range of US$1,600-3,000.)

   Bookstore. A tiny, unnumbered shop featuring old Chinese books, including outsized art books with reproductions.

92 **Lantern shop.** Lanterns may be made to order from a selection of materials on hand.

80 **Peking Antiquity Shop.** Specializing in old porcelains, its stock has been well picked-over by connoisseurs, although it still carries one of the best selections in China. Poking through the jumbled cases at least provides the illusion of discovery. Aging (if not antique) scrolls (US $30-200) and prints (US $5-10) are also offered for sale.

70 **Peking Antiquity Shop.** This is more an "odds and ends" store, but offers curiosities such as old jewelry, leather boxes, and cloisonné.

63 **Scroll shop.** Sells both old and new scrolls and paintings. Also has painted fans, books of paintings, and antique clothing and brocades.

60 **Chop store.** Prices often mystify first-time shoppers. Although the aesthetic criteria may seem obscure, some stones are simply deemed rarer than others. No sentimentality is lost on their former owners and chops can be re-engraved on request.

Doubling back and crossing to the west side of Liu Li Ch'ang, there are three shops of interest:

20 **Chop and rubbing shop.** Features excellent-quality old rubbings and chops. While most chops and some rubbings are out in the display cases, the walls are lined with shelves carrying thousands of old rubbings. The problem is that one must know what one wants (e.g., particular calligraphers, styles of calligraphy, certain historical figures), since the shop staff is reluctant to expend their time in aimless searches. Ink stones and silver cigarette boxes are also sold here.

19 **Stationery and supply shop.** Newly opened (1976), this store carries everything from blank cards with peasant paintings on them to inkstones and brushes. Oil paintings (many not for sale) and reproductions line the walls. The shop's most fascinating aspect is what it "hides." Behind the store is a labyrinth of workshops that turn out the reproductions, original paintings, and fine crafts displayed in front. Even if a special trip is required, a visit here is especially recommended.

31 **Scroll-making shop.** Workers here will mount a favorite painting or rubbing on a scroll. (Costs vary greatly depending on the style and materials chosen.)

Tientsin

entrance to the heavenly capital
Pinyin: Tianjin ("teean-jin")

Tientsin, China's third largest city, is located some 120 km. (74 mi.) southeast of Peking and 50 km. (30 mi.) from the Pohai Gulf. It possesses China's largest artificial harbor and is a key transportation hub serving the populous North China Plain. The city is also a leading industrial center.

Tientsin has a population of 6.7 million spread over an area of 11,000 sq.km. (4,200 sq.mi.) and is one of China's three centrally-administered municipalities (with Peking and Shanghai). Tientsin proper extends for almost 10 miles along the banks of the Hai River, a factor which in the past made the city (with an average elevation of 16 ft.) constantly vulnerable to flooding. In recent years, water control projects have all but eliminated this threat.

Tientsin in History

Recently unearthed records indicate that Tientsin's original site dates back to the Warring States period (403-221 BC). However, continuous occupation apparently did not begin until about 800 years ago, when the city was known as Chih-ku ("buying and selling"). Tientsin received its present name in 1404, at a time when it began to assume its characteristic role as a transshipment point between the southern coast and Peking. A military garrison was posted, city walls built (destroyed during the Boxer Rebellion), and storage facilities expanded. The next phase of Tientsin's development began in 1858 when the city was designated as a treaty port. The city was parcelled out among British, French, and other Western concessions. Western-style buildings were constructed, port facilities improved, and light industry (mostly textiles) expanded.

Early in this century, the heavy silting of the Hai River forced the rebuilding of the port 50 km. downstream from the city of Taiku. During the Japanese occupation (1937-45), a major construction program was begun to construct an artificial harbor and deep-water berthing facilities. These were completed under the PRC in 1952. A second major expansion, including containerization, was carried out in 1976.

The city suffered heavy damage during the Tangshan Earthquake (1976) but by 1978, full production had been restored and tourists were once again allowed to visit the city.

Economy and Culture

Tientsin's economy is dominated by its port and heavy industry. Ships up to 10,000 tons can berth in the new artificial port, with ships up to 3,000 tons serving Tientsin itself. Heavy industry includes iron and steel, motor vehicles and parts, heavy machinery, chemicals, electronics, and watches. Tientsin-made elevators are used in hotels and office buildings throughout China.

Perhaps its most famous products are Tientsin carpets. Eight major factories produce an estimated 150,000 sq.yd. of carpet annually.

The area is also rich in natural resources. Some of China's largest coal mines are in nearby Tangshan. The major Shengli oil field is now being supplemented by extensive new offshore discoveries. In agriculture, Tientsin produces wheat, corn, and rice and has a thriving dairy industry. Fruit is also grown, and pears are notable.

HIGHLIGHTS FOR TRAVELERS

The Number One Carpet Factory employs 1,400 workers, two-thirds of whom are women. This industry dates back to 200 BC in China. For Tientsin carpets no weaving machinery is used. To impart an embossed effect, designs are etched with scissors.

The Hai River caused a major flood in 1963, and since then major water-control projects have been underway, including construction of new streams (to bypass the river), locks, and pumping stations.

Other sites of interest include a terra-cotta ceramics factory (the figures make excellent souvenirs), several large parks (Shuishang Park contains a museum with Ming and Ch'ing dynasty paintings), and the old city with its maze of narrow streets and bazaars.

Talien

great link
Pinyin Spelling: Dalian ("dah-leean")

Talien (formerly known in the west as "Dairen") lies at the southern tip of the Liaotung Peninsula in northeast China. It is the country's third largest port engaging in foreign trade. Although the city is located 500 km. (310 mi.) due east of Peking, the train route must cover an additional 1,450 km. (900 mi.) in its journey around the Pohai Gulf.

The city has broad streets and spacious squares, and is known both for its industry and its scenic setting. Rounded, green hills form the backdrop on three sides. The deep blue bay to the south is skirted by four excellent beaches. The main industrial zone has been built in the suburbs to alleviate crowding in the city.

Talien in History

Construction of Talien's port began in 1899 and was completed in 1930 by the Japanese. Under terms of the 1945 Yalta Conference, con-

trol of the city passed from Japan to the Soviet Union, which occupied
the city until the early 1950s (ironically, it was the Soviets who helped
complete Talien's vast network of underground defense shelters). The
Soviet presence still lingers as evidenced by the bilingual street signs
and cenotaph with Russian and Chinese inscriptions that dominates
Stalin Square at the city's center.

HIGHLIGHTS FOR TRAVELERS

On the way to Talien, the train passes through fields of sorghum and
soybeans. The outskirts of the city are dominated by factories that
produce diesel engines, ships, metals, chemicals, textiles, refinery
products, processed food, and blown glass. The city is the second
most important cultural center in Liaoning Province (after Shenyang). In addition to its university there is a teachers' college, technical institute, and agricultural college.

Sightseeing in Talien usually includes the port, some factories,
and the beach resorts. The port employs about 13% of the population
and its ice-free harbor receives ships from over 100 countries. Modern
dock facilities can handle containerized shipping and oil and coal
from northeast China. In addition to touring the factories themselves,
visitors are often taken to see new residential neighborhoods for
workers, affording a view of daily life in the city. Recreational areas
such as Tiger Park (Laohutan) are quite popular, especially in the
summer.

Anshan

Anshan, the steel capital of China, is located in Liaoning Province about 80 km. (50 mi.) southwest of Shenyang. The city is set amidst a densely populated agricultural-industrial area rich in deposits of iron and coal. Anshan boasts the largest iron and steel complex in China (although Wuhan is more modern and may soon supplant it). It produces about one-fourth of China's steel. The Chinese are especially proud of Anshan because of its role in providing most of the steel used in the PRC's initial industrial expansion during the 1950s.

Appropriately enough, the town is on the same latitude as a US steel center, Youngstown, Ohio. Its climate, however, is more like that of Minneapolis: hot, dry summers and bitter winters, when the temperature rarely goes above freezing.

Anshan in History. Iron and steel are also synonymous with the history of Anshan. Organized iron mining and smelting began about 100 BC. There was some expansion of activity during the 10th and 11th centuries, but during the Ch'ing Dynasty a superstitious Manchu emperor curtailed operations for fear of disturbing some ancestral graves about 10 miles away.

The modern development of Anshan began with the rediscovery of iron ore deposits by the Japanese in the early 1900s. The Japanese added the first open-hearth furnaces in 1935.

Anshan was occupied by the Soviet army in 1945, which immediately began the systematic dismantling and removal of power-generating and transforming equipment, electric motors, and the newest and best machine tools. Anshan's condition worsened during the civil war (1946-49), when control of the town seesawed back and forth 11 times between the Communists and the Kuomintang. The Red Army finally gained permanent control in 1948, whereupon restoration of the iron and steel plant was given the highest priority.

Highlights for Travelers

Today, the iron and steel plant sprawls over an area of about 5 sq. mi., monopolizing the skyline of the northwest part of the city with its belching smoke stacks, blast furnaces, and cooling towers.

In addition to iron and steel, Anshan produces agricultural machinery, construction materials, chemicals, and consumer goods. There are several parks, schools, and technical institutes (mostly related to the metallurgical industry). A hot spring lies about 6 miles southeast of the city.

Anshan possesses few sights of historical interest, although the house of the former warlord Chang Tso-lin (d. 1928) is located here, as is the home of Henry P'u-yi, the last Ch'ing emperor who for a while served as the puppet Emperor K'ang-te of "Manchukuo" under the Japanese.

NORTHERN CHINA

Shenyang　沈陽

north of the river Shen
Pinyin Spelling: Shenyang ("shen-yong")

Shenyang, the capital of Liaoning Province, is a large industrial city with 3 million people. Formerly called "Mukden" (its name in the Manchurian language), it is the communications hub and industrial center of northeast China.

China's Northeast Region (Tung-pei), comprising the three provinces of Liaoning, Kirin, and Heilungkiang, was for centuries little more than a barren steppe sparsely populated by herdsmen. The discovery by Westerners in the 19th century that this part of Manchuria was the repository of vast natural resources brought rapid changes. At the same time, the region became a focal point of foreign contention and rapacity. The Japanese set up a puppet government there in 1932, calling the region "Manchukuo," and launched into large-scale coal mining. At the end of World War II, the Soviets sought unsuccessfully to fill the political and military void left by the defeated Japanese.

Since 1949, the region has been methodically developed, with activities focusing around Shenyang (steel) and Harbin (oil). Liaoning Province is still relatively underpopulated. Nevertheless, Shenyang's growth is underscored by the fact that in 1910 it had only 100,000 people. Today its wide tree-lined streets, tall buildings, and spacious squares lend an appearance more suggestive of the West than many Chinese cities. The city is located 841 km. (522 mi.) northeast of Peking by rail (the express train takes 12 hours; jet flights, about one and a half hours). The best time of year to visit Shenyang is in the summer. Winters are bitterly cold.

Shenyang in History

Although the origins of Shenyang can be traced back some 2,000 years, it did not emerge as a city of note until the 11th century when, under the Mongol (Yuan) Dynasty, it thrived as a trading center for nomads. Among the powerful tribes in the region were the Manchus (the origin of the name is obscure) who began their rise to power by conquering and politically consolidating the northern border lands in the early 17th century. Murhachi (1559-1626), founder of the Manchu state, began his open war against China's Ming rulers in 1618. By 1625, he controlled enough of the northern region to be able to establish a capital at Shenyang. In 1636, his 14th son and successor, Dorgon, proclaimed the founding of the Ch'ing ("pure") Dynasty from Shenyang. Peking was finally seized in 1644 after a Chinese commander had literally invited the Manchus inside the Great Wall. Mukden remained a secondary capital, however, in part because the rulers did not want to give up the lucrative ginseng trade —the Manchu equivalent of the salt monopolies established under the Ming.

Shenyang played a role in the Boxer Rebellion of 1900 and was the site of a 17-day battle during the Russo-Japanese War of 1902-05. In 1932, the Japanese established military control over Manchuria. They created the independent state of Manchukuo, installing the last Ch'ing Emperor, Henry Pu'yi, as regent (the "Mukden Incident").

The Japanese converted the area into an industrial base, with virtually all resources funnelled off to the motherland.

The city was renamed Shenyang in 1949. The PRC government continues to eschew reference to the former names of Manchuria and Mukden.

Economy and Culture

Shenyang, as the largest city in northeastern China, supports a diversified array of heavy industry. Major enterprises include electrical equipment (e.g., high-voltage transformers), machine building, metallurgy, chemicals, textiles, and food processing.

Efforts to make Shenyang agriculturally self-reliant have been stepped-up, and the dry northern terrain now yields soybeans, cotton, tobacco, peanuts, apples, and pears. Afforestation is also a major undertaking; and there are two large nurseries in the area.

The city itself has a home for aged workers, a Workers Cultural Palace, and 12 parks featuring numerous small lakes. Education facilities include the provincial university, several technical institutes, and a large medical institute. Extensive day-care and health-care facilities have been set up adjacent to factories.

The most famous cultural institution in Shenyang is its acrobatic troupe. Such forms of entertainment have been popular in China for centuries (acrobats were depicted in tomb figures as early as the T'ang Dynasty) and are today actively supported by the government. Although most of the major cities have their own troupes, the Shenyang group—which maintains its own school, dormitories, and training facilities—is better known in the West because of its tours (including one to North America in 1973).

HIGHLIGHTS FOR TRAVELERS

The principal incentive for a visit to Shenyang is the chance to see something of China's industrial development. In addition, the local branch of CITS will include a tour of the city's historical points of interest.

☐ **The Imperial Palace.** When the Manchus established their capital in Shenyang in 1625, the first order of business was to build a proper palace. The result was a complex of some 70 buildings, occupying a space of 50,000 sq. m. (59,800 sq. yd.), and replete with lacquered roof tiles. The project was completed in 1637.

After the Manchus moved their capital to Peking, the Shenyang palace was kept up, serving as the second seat of power in the empire. The library (Wen Shu Gallery) once held 35,533 volumes, including a massive history of China completed in 1782.

Today, visitors still file past the stone tablets written in Chinese, Manchurian, Mongolian, Arabic, and Tibetan, informing those who enter that they must dismount from their horses before being admitted. The exhibits include the personal effects of the Ch'ien Lung Emperor (1736-96) and an assortment of bows, arrows, musical instruments, dresses, pottery, porcelain, carvings, and a bell weighing over four tons.

☐ **North Tomb (Pei Ling).** The tomb bears the remains of Abukai (1592-1643), the founder of the Manchu Dynasty, and his wife. Succeeding Ch'ing emperors came here to pay homage to their ancestors. By the 19th century, however, the tomb had fallen into disrepair. Since 1949, it has been restored and a large park built around it with lakes, pavilions, and a forest of trees. In the style of the Ming emperors, animal statues line the walkway to the tomb and a stele is inscribed with Abukai's calligraphy. There is a hall of ancestors and an inner court with the burial mound lying just beyond.

☐ **East Tomb (Tung Ling).** Located about 8 km. (5 mi.) east of Shenyang on the banks of the Shen River, this site is the tomb of Nurhachi, the father of Abukai. Nurhachi (who was given the posthumous title of T'ai Tsu—"grand progenitor") was a gifted leader, military commander, and scholar. His tomb is similar to that of his son, but less grand and less often visited. It was completed in 1626, a year after his death.

☐ **Liaoning Exhibition Center.** The Liaoning Exhibition Center, located in the southern section of the city, was built in the late 1950s in Soviet architectural style. With 41,800 sq. m. of display space, it was officially opened to the public in 1960. The exhibit is continually updated with new industrial products turned out in the Shenyang area.

HOTEL ACCOMMODATIONS

Shenyang's only hotel, formerly known as the Mukden Railway Hotel, is the Liaoning Guest House. It has high ceilings, wide corridors, and a marble lobby, making it something of a landmark in its own right. During the 1940s, it served as a meeting place for representatives of contending political factions in China's civil war. Among the more tangible legacies of those days are some of the finest slate billiard tables found in China.

The hotel, whose rates are Y22 per day, has the standard tourist amenities: bank, post office, and retail shop. It is located at Sun Yat-sen Square, affording ideal access to the center of the city.

SHENYANG CUISINE

The cooking of northern China is not as elaborate as in other parts of China, but the region has a famous dish said to have originated with the Mongols: Hou Kuo ("fire pot"). A charcoal brazier is placed on the table and water boiled. While the water is heating, the service workers will prepare a sauce from rice wine, vinegar, chili sauce, sesame oil, shrimp paste, and soy sauce. Plates of raw meat (beef, mutton, chicken, and, perhaps, a surprise or two), sliced razor thin, are placed around the table. Guests then cook their own meat. The pieces are dipped in the sauce before eating. The meats are followed by vegetables and, lastly, noodles. By the end of this sequence, the water has been transformed into a rich, flavorful broth.

SHOPPING

Handicrafts from Shenyang are relatively undistinguished. Fur items are the favored local purchases. There is an antique store in Taiyan Street, with a rather limited selection. Overseas Chinese prefer to purchase ginseng and antler powders here, both indigenous to the area.

Constructing a New Refinery

Harbin

Pinyin Spelling: Harbin

Harbin is an industrial and rail center situated in the far northeast of China. It sits on salty, semi-arid lands, with winter temperatures falling below –40° C (–40° F). The capital of Heilungkiang Province, it is located 694 miles north of Peking by rail, a journey consuming about 19 hours (4 hours by air). Its population is 1.5 million.

Harbin, founded at the turn of the century, has little of historical interest. Within the context of modern China, however, it is a site of major significance owing to the presence of the Taching oilfields, the foremost national model for industrial development.

Taching

The story of Taching begins in the 1930s when Japanese geologists detected large oil reserves in the highland plains. After the founding of the PRC in 1949, exploratory drilling began with technical assistance from the Soviet Union. In 1959, before the work could produce results, Soviet technicians were withdrawn as a consequence of the Sino-Soviet split. Despite severe shortcomings in technology, the Chinese pressed on. By means of massive labor inputs and grass roots ingenuity and tenacity (as exemplified by "Iron Man" Wang and other workers now regarded as national heroes), they completed work on what was to become one of China's greatest natural resources and a major boost to the country's economic transformation. In 1964, Chairman Mao coined the slogan "In industry, learn from Taching," still used as the national rallying-cry for industrial development. For the Chinese, its image conjures up the ultimate example of worker discipline, skillful planning, managerial efficiency, and the triumph of spirit over circumstance.

Since 1960, production is said to have increased by an annual average of 28% (despite slowdowns in the mid-1970s attributed to political disruptions by the "gang of four"), reaching an estimated level of 40 million metric tons (280 million barrels) in 1977. Local crude oil contains high quantities of parafin and is too viscous to flow at cold temperatures. As a result, many of the pipes and storage tanks are buried underground. The Taching complex itself (actually made up of two fields) spreads over 1,000 sq. km. (386 sq. mi.).

In a style now emulated throughout China, Taching has not limited itself to a single activity, but rather has developed into a multifaceted agro-industrial complex. It now comprises a constellation of over 50 villages where wives and families of oil workers farm 2,300 hectares (5,543 acres) of land to supply food and auxiliary sources of income for the region. Schools, nurseries, medical centers, and universities form an integral part of the complex.

NORTHERN CHINA

Changchun

eternal spring

Pinyin Spelling: Changchun ("chang-jewn")

Changchun, the capital of Kirin Province, is situated on the Yitung River in the central part of the Northeast Plain. A city of 1.5 million, it is primarily known as the first center of China's automotive industry.

Changchun is characterized by wide, tree-lined avenues and large administrative buildings. Much of the present city was constructed between 1933 and 1945, when, as part of the Manchurian region occupied by Japan, it was designated the capital of "Manchukuo."

In 1953, work on China's first automobile factory began in Changchun. The plant has since undergone several phases of expansion and now produces trucks and automobiles, including the famous "Red Flag" limousines. The city's industry also includes machine tools, railway cars, electric motors, textiles, and food processing.

There are two hotels in Changchun. In addition to the industrial sites, tourists are likely to have a chance to visit Kirin University and one of China's largest film studios.

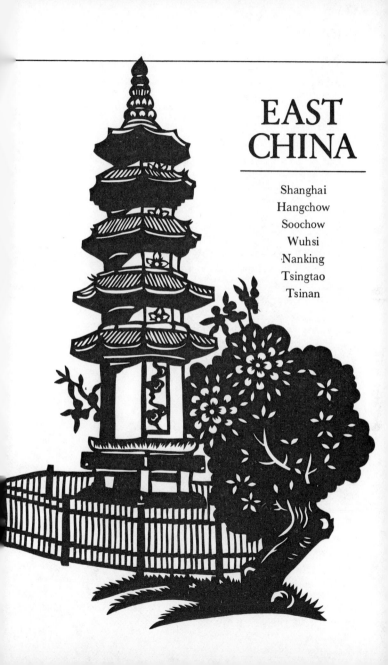

EAST CHINA

Shanghai
Hangchow
Soochow
Wuhsi
Nanking
Tsingtao
Tsinan

Shanghai

up from the sea
Pinyin Spelling: Shanghai ("shong-high")

Shanghai is China's most populous city and its largest in area, covering 6,100 sq.km. (2,355 sq.mi.) overall and supporting a population of some 10.8 million. About 5.6 million people live in the congested urban core, which covers an area of 143 sq.km. (55 sq.mi.).

Shanghai is one of three large cities administered directly by the central government (Tientsin and Peking are the other two). Its political importance is underscored by the traditionally high proportion of its citizens in chief government and Party posts in Peking. It is divided into 10 districts, which are in turn divided into 80 neighborhood units.

Shanghai is the center of China's trade and industry. Almost half of the country's entire internal and external commerce passes through the city, conveyed by ocean vessels, river craft, airplanes, and railroads. Situated on the Whangpoo River, it lies 12 miles upstream from the mighty Yangtse River. The Yangtse in turn links Shanghai to the Pacific Ocean on the east and to the interior cities of Nanking, Wuhan, and Chengtu. Shanghai is served by four airports, two of which are civil. Hung Chiao Airport is the principal link for international and domestic travel. The main railway station, with its huge freight yards, is in the north-central section of the city.

Shanghai has the most Western European look of any Chinese city. Its urban and industrial growth occurred while under the domination of Western powers. The famous Bund—Shanghai's bustling boulevard along the west bank of the Whangpoo—presents an impressive skyline of tall buildings. Once hotels, clubs, banks, and offices for foreigners, they now house municipal offices, branches of PRC foreign trade corporations, a customs house, and two hotels.

South and west of the downtown area the architecture is more typically Chinese, with low-lying, close-quartered buildings, small shops, and busy markets. The architecture of the north section of the city still bears evidence of the former Japanese concession. Along much of the waterfront in the outlying areas are sizable industrial districts, with many of the newer developments surrounded by workers' apartment blocks. The newest section of Shanghai is in its southwest corner. Here, an impressive indoor stadium has been built along with several high-rise apartment buildings.

The climate of Shanghai is temperate, with hot and humid summers (and usually considerable rain), and winters that can be chilly and grey. Spring and autumn are the most comfortable seasons with pleasant temperatures and infrequent precipitation.

Shanghai in History

Compared to most other major cities of China, Shanghai's history has been short and, until the last century, relatively uneventful. In the 11th century, it was a fishing village built atop some isolated mud flats. During the 17th and 18th centuries, with the development of silk and cotton production in the surrounding areas, it became more of a trading center. By the early 1800s, it was a flourishing domestic port of some 50,000 people.

Significant growth did not occur until the arrival of Europeans in the mid-19th century. In 1842, near the end of the Opium War, Shanghai's garrison surrendered to the British fleet. From that point until 1949 the city developed largely as an enclave for Western commercial interests in China. Lying off the sea and just upstream from the Yangtse—a river that could be navigated several hundred miles into the interior on oceangoing vessels—Shanghai provided a gateway to a vast internal market. Each of the major foreign powers claimed a section of the city. Residents of these infamous "international concessions" were exempt from the laws of China and Chinese were subjected to the added humiliation of being barred from free access to portions of their own territory. Shanghai soon surpassed Kwangchow as China's most important foreign trade center. Numerous traders and speculators—French, US, and Japanese—soon joined the British. By 1936, the Western population of Shanghai had reached 60,000.

Shanghai in the Revolution. While Western merchants prospered and Shanghai's export-oriented industry and commerce flourished, the city spawned vast urban slums. Gradually, these conditions prompted growing discontent, strikes, and revolts against foreign rule and influence. In 1921, the Chinese Communist Party was founded in Shanghai. In 1925, the Party helped carry out the demonstrations and strikes known as the May 30th Movement. A year later, workers organized an armed uprising, but it was bloodily suppressed by Chiang Kai-shek's Nationalist troops in 1927. During the 1930s, Shanghai was relatively quiet as the revolutionary movement changed its focus to the countryside. By the 1940s, it had earned the reputation as an "adventurer's paradise." Under its glittering surface festered opium dens, brothels, crime syndicates, and rampant corruption. During the World War II, the city was occupied by the Japanese . In May 1949, following a brief revival of Nationalist rule, the Red Army triumphantly entered the city.

Since then, Shanghai has shed itself of crime, foreign exploitation, and all vestiges of its former decadence. Today, the neon signs remain to extol Marxist values. Questions about the "old days" are usually met with awkward silence, as if the visitor were probing into the sooner forgotten misdeeds of a wayward child.

Economy and Culture

The Chinese are quick to point out that since 1949 Shanghai has shed its identity as a center of consumption. No longer a drain on the national economy, it is now one of its chief sources of production. Before 1949, Shanghai's economy was fueled largely by commerce, with some light industry and textiles. Today, it supports nearly 10,000 factories. Industrial output is 18.3 times greater than that of 1949 and the city's share of heavy industry in the gross national product has

Whangpoo River, Shanghai

1 Hsi Chao Park
2 Lung Hua Temple
3 Shanghai Children's Palace
4 Shanghai Industrial Exhibition
5 Chin Chiang Hotel
6 Fu Hsing Park
7 Shanghai Radio and Television Tower
8 Site of Founding of Chinese Communist Party
9 International Hotel
10 People's Park
11 People's Square
12 Workers Cultural Palace
13 No. 1 Department Store
14 Shanghai Museum of Art and History
15 Garden of Yu
16 Lu Hsun Memorial Park
17 Peace Hotel
18 Friendship Store
19 Shanghai Mansions Hotel
20 Shanghai No. 1 Hospital
21 Shanghai Harbor

risen from 13.6% to 53.4%. Shanghai now produces significant quantities of iron and steel (some 1,000 types of specialty steel for 20,000 different products), heavy machinery, chemicals, electrical equipment, motor vehicles, ships (up to 10,000 tons), tires, paper, and glassware. Petrochemical plants and oil refineries line the Whangpoo River. In the first half of 1977, Shanghai handled 34% of the country's seagoing freight. The port has recently been expanded and is now capable of handling containerized cargo.

About 2.5 million people are employed in the industrial sector, earning an average monthly wage of about Y65 (US $38.25), which includes the pay raise given to 60% of China's workforce in late 1977. Family income averages Y100-150 (US $58-88) per month, of which about 5% is taken by rent and 8-15% by food.

Improvements in living standards include new housing projects that have increased residential floorspace by 15 million sq. m. (18 million sq. yd.). There are two elevated railways with a subway nearing completion (the harbor tunnels have already been set in place). Shanghai's inhabitants own 1.1 million bicycles—a figure second only to Peking's.

Although agriculture plays a less prominent role in Shanghai's economy, output from surrounding farmlands meets the municipality's requirements for vegetables and cooking oil and have made it

Ship-Launching, Shanghai

nearly self-sufficient in total food needs. Some 360,000 hectares (889,560 acres) are cultivated, yielding four times the output of the early 1950s. Suburbs of Shanghai boast 200 communes, producing crops such as rice, cotton, vegetables, grain, poultry, livestock, and fish. It is a model area for farm mechanization, where progress has been especially evident in the mid-1970s.

Shanghai also considers itself the leading cultural and educational center of China and in this regard carries on a friendly rivalry with Peking. There are a number of outstanding ballet and opera companies, symphonies, puppet troops, acrobats, and a circus. Its reputation as a literary center has been enhanced by famous writers such as Lu Hsun, whose powerful accounts of misery and corruption in the city during the 1930s are now regarded as classics of modern Chinese fiction.

Futan University, specializing in the sciences, is Shanghai's leading institution of higher learning. The city pioneered in the creation of part-time schools at factories where workers are trained in technical skills. At the Shanghai Science and Technical Exchange, industrial workers from different sectors meet to exchange scientific and technical information (as of September 1977, it had 1,500 members working in 22 teams). Shanghai is also important for medical training. A world-famous team of doctors at the Number 6 Hospital specializes in the reattachment of severed limbs. Shanghai also has a teaching hospital for foreign doctors seeking to learn acupuncture.

HIGHLIGHTS FOR TRAVELERS

While Shanghai is one of the most fascinating cities in the world, it is not particularly endowed with historical attractions—there are no great architectural landmarks or archaeological sites. Rather, Shanghai has become a place where visitors may vividly come to grips with the ways in which China functions today. Shanghai's new housing projects for workers offer insight into how China is organized politically and socially at the neighborhood level; factories demonstrate the role of management teams. The local agricultural communes have achieved impressive levels of diversity (and prosperity).

☐ **People's Square and People's Park.** Occupying an area of about 1 sq. mi. in the heart of the city are the People's Square and the adjoining People's Park. The area was originally laid out in 1861 by a foreigner who traced a large oval on horseback with a sword and then bought up everything within it (including farmland and buildings) to build a park and a race course. The racetrack has now been replaced by a pleasant park with lawns, ponds, and tree-shaded walkways. The large, 35-hectare (86-acre) square to the south is used for celebrations, processions, and political rallies. An interesting historical museum is located within the park grounds. It houses ceramic figures, bronzes, jade objects, and some tortoise plastrons (in ancient times, heat was applied to the shells, producing cracks that were used to divine the future).

☐ **Fu Hsing Park.** This 8.77-hectare (21.7-acre) park, located in the south-central section of the city, was built in 1909. It is notable for its massive trees with foliage so dense that the hot summer sun hardly penetrates, and for a small zoo (Shanghai's main zoo is in Hsi Chao Park). The park offers a convenient airing for residents of the nearby Chin Chiang Hotel. It is often filled with older people playing Chinese chess and minding the grandchildren. Nearby is the former residence of Sun Yat-sen. It is maintained as a small museum.

☐ **Hsi Chao Park (Western Suburbs Park).** Although it is rarely part of the tourist's formal itinerary, this park is delightful to explore on one's own (if there is a half-day's free time). As its name implies, it is located on the western edge of the city and is near Hung Chiao Airport. The park contains a number of small lakes (e.g., Swan Lake), small pavilions, a children's playground, an open-air theater, and a skating rink. The Shanghai Zoo is also located here, boasting 400 species of animals living in as natural an environment as possible.

☐ **Lu Hsun Memorial Park.** Lu Hsun (1881-36), one of China's most famous modern writers, used to walk through this park, located in the northeastern section of the city. His grave is in the park, marked by a steel statue erected in 1961. In the garden surrounding the grave are two trees: one planted by Madame Lu, the other by Chou En-lai. The calligraphy at the site is by Mao Tse-tung. A Lu Hsun Museum contains photographs, letters, manuscripts, furniture, and other memorabilia.

☐ **Shanghai Museum of Art and History.** Less well known than the Municipal Museum (perhaps because it is less accessible), this museum houses the best art works in Shanghai, if not in all of central China. It has a stunning collection of bronzes and the quality of its paintings (especially from the Sung and T'ang dynasties) is unsurpassed anywhere in the country. The bronze artifacts include a huge *ting* (three-legged cauldron) and a rich collection of ritual vessels, tools, and mirrors. The exhibits rotate.

☐ **Lung Hua Temple District.** This scenic district in the southwestern suburbs of Shanghai is renowned for its peach blossoms, pagoda, and temple. The seven-tiered Lung Hua Pagoda was first built in 247 AD and reconstructed during the Sung Dynasty. The pagoda was a popular site for foreigners during the first half of this century. The source of fascination was its slight tilt. It was fully restored in 1954, with small bronze bells hung from its numerous eaves. The temple features a 10-ft. statue of a laughing Buddha and others of Buddha's disciples. A neighboring palace features a 3,300-lb. bronze clock built in 1382.

☐ **Garden of the Mandarin Yu (Yu Yuan).** The old section of Shanghai, which is just south of the central shopping and business district, is demarcated on the map by the ring road. It used to have an unsavory reputation among foreigners living in Shanghai, since only Chinese could wander through in safety. These days it is perfectly safe, although the visitor is likely to be followed at a discreet distance by curious school children, who find great humor in visitors' frequent turns into blind alleys.

It was here that a city official named Yu built a garden in the late 16th century (Ming Dynasty). A small lake has a zig-zag bridge, teahouse, terraces, and pavilions. This site was the headquarters of the Small Sword Society, which led an uprising in 1853 against the foreign presence in Shanghai.

☐ **Workers Cultural Palace.** Pre-1949 guide books wistfully refer to the Ta Shih Chieh (Great World) entertainment center, which once comprised ten theaters, a circus, and other forms of amusement. Today, the site is occupied by the Workers Cultural Palace. It is closed to foreigners except during the yearly commemoration of Chairman Mao's "Talk on Art and Literature at the Yenan Forum," when all theaters in Shanghai burst forth with plays, operas, ballets, dance dramas, and other forms of entertainment for the people.

☐ **Shanghai Industrial Exhibition.** This large exhibition hall is sure to be included on any visitor's itinerary. Built by the Soviets in the early 1950s, it was formerly called the Palace of Sino-Soviet Friendship. Over 5,000 industrial and consumer products are on display, from mechanical rice harvesters to precision grinding machines, from heavy construction equipment to small toys that intone a song usually associated with Disneyland, "It's a Small World Everywhere."

☐ **Children's Palace.** Children between the ages of 7 and 17 who show particular skills in subjects such as dance, music, mechanics, and mathematics have an opportunity to receive part-time specialized training at "children's palaces." These schools have excellent facilities, with instruction often provided by leading professional artists. There are seven such palaces in Shanghai. The largest is on Yenan Road near the Industrial Exhibition. It is also the city's first such institution, converted in 1949 from a mansion that belonged to a foreign businessman. The concept (with roots in the Soviet Union) was promoted in China by Soong Ching-ling, Sun Yat-sen's daughter, who has held honorific positions in the government since 1949.

☐ **Worker's New Residential Areas.** Eleven new housing districts on the outskirts of Shanghai are readily identified on Chinese maps. Visitors are usually taken to one of three. Such visits are important facets of any visit to China since they serve to demonstrate the impact of political, social, and economic changes on the lives of ordinary citizens.

Most of these areas were built around large factory sites on the outskirts of the city so as to alleviate crowding in central Shanghai and to avoid putting additional strains on the transportation system for commuters. Politically, these units operate at the "neighborhood" level of Shanghai's administration, with each local unit's committee exercising authority over the building of schools, shops, and nurseries, as well as recreation and medical services.

The Chao Yang residential area, Shanghai's first, was built in 1951. It has been expanded several times and now occupies some 200 hectares (494 acres). Housing consists mainly of 2- to 5-story apartment buildings. In 1977, Chao Yang had 72,000 residents distributed among 17,800 households. The area has 8 middle schools, 9 elementary schools, 7 kindergartens, and 8 nurseries. There are 2 hospitals and 12 cooperative public health stations. Other amenities include a cinema, park, bookstore, shopping center, post office, public baths, and a department store.

Visitors are usually taken to see a worker's apartment. A retired worker (aged 60) visited in 1973 paid a monthly rent of Y5 (US $3.20). His retirement income was Y104 (US.$61) per month, or 70% of his last salary. A return visit in 1977 showed the addition of a television set, a new sewing machine, and a sofa ("my wife asked for it"). Typically, the apartment had a living area and a bedroom. Its kitchen was shared by one other family.

□ **Futan University.** Educational policies implemented after Mao's death and the demise of the "gang of four" have included the first administration of university entrance examinations since the Cultural Revolution (1966). In 1978, broad reforms were still taking place. Futan University, often identified with "radical" educational policies in the past, was expected to undergo dramatic changes as a result of these new policies.

The university was founded in 1905 and now has 14 departments, including foreign languages, international politics, history, chemistry, physics, mathematics, genetics, and atomic energy. In early 1977, it had 4,100 students and a teaching staff of 2,000. Overall, about two-thirds of the students specialized in the sciences, the remainder in the arts and humanities.

□ **Factories.** Factories included on the visitor's itinerary are frequently those producing electrical turbines, buses, diesel engines, and toys. Shanghai Machine Tool Plant No. 1 is among the most famous units in China, having been designated as a model factory by Chairman Mao himself in the 1960s. Its output typifies the progress China has been making in building automated and semi-automated precision tools. The plant employs 6,000 workers who earn an average of Y68 (US$40) per month, with the highest worker's wage set at Y124 and the lowest, Y42. Technical and administrative personnel receive up to Y250 (US$147) per month. In addition, all employees receive subsidies for health care, commuting, and other items.

Of special pride to the Machine Tools Factory are its three schools for training technicians from among the workers. The system developed here is regarded as a national model. Workers who reach a certain level of skill and political status may enroll in these schools. Afterwards, they are often transferred to factories in different parts of China so as to pass on their skills in regions where they are most needed.

WALKING TOURS

Shanghai's outgoing residents love to take long walks, especially along the riverfront. For those up on their PRC geography, a simple guideline for getting around is to remember that the east-west streets in the center of town are named after Chinese cities (e.g., Nanking, Peking); north-south streets are named after provinces. The walks that follow originate at the Peace Hotel.

□ **The Bund** (30 minutes or more). It may seem unnecessary to note that a street has two sides; yet, Chung Shan Road—the name now given to the Bund—acts much as a boundary between two separate worlds. On the eastern side is the river, fronted by a long, narrow park. Here, Shanghai residents relax, walk along the river, perform *t'ai ch'i ch'uan* (in the early mornings), and hold hands and whisper quietly (in the evenings). The western side is all business. People hurry along, darting in and out of the office buildings that line the road.

Proceeding left from the Peace Hotel along Chung Shan Road, one passes buildings that formerly housed Japanese and US banks, now the office of branches of China's foreign trade corporations. Crossing Peking Road, still heading north, a low wall marks the grounds of the Friendship Store and the seaman's club (not open to visitors). This was formerly the compound of the British Consulate. The Friendship Store, once occupying three buildings, has been consolidated to make way for new construction. A new Friendship Store was scheduled to be built during 1978-79.

Just before Soochow Creek and the Garden Bridge is a small park favored for morning exercises and evening gossip. After walking to the middle of the bridge (for a view of the river traffic), return (walking south) along the western side of the street. Here is the park with its comfortable benches, small flower beds, and shade trees. Along the river is a concrete wall—perfect for reclining, taking pictures, and watching the changing river scenery. Follow the river bank south to the old weather station at Yenan Road; the guy wires formerly used for hoisting different colored flags to indicate changes in the weather are still there. Cross the street and return northward.

There is another seaman's club at the corner of Kwangtung Road, just before the famous Customs House, with its bell tower that used to chime out "The East is Red." At the northern corner of Foochow Road, two bronze lions still stand astride an immense doorway to the old headquarters of the Hong Kong and Shanghai Banking Corporation. The building has been renovated and its use radically transformed to house the municipal headquarters of Shanghai. The Peace Hotel is two short blocks away.

☐ **The Old Chinese City** (2 hours or more). South along the Bund past Yenan Road lies a part of the city with a totally different look. The colonnaded buildings give way to block offices and low-slung dwellings, and the orderliness of the Bund gives way to more typical waterfront disorder.

After Yenan Road the first main street is Chinling Lu, followed by Ren Min Road. Continue two more blocks until reaching Fuyu Lu, and turn right (west) into Shanghai's old Chinese quarter. This street first crosses Ren Min Road (which is circular) and then, a short block later, Tan Feng Lu. It veers slightly right and then crosses An Jen Chieh. Here is the Yu Yuan Garden.

One can either continue exploring the area (the many small lanes at odd angles make it easy to lose one's way) or retrace the same route back. Alternatively, continue one block further west to Szechuan (also spelled Ssu Ch'uan) Road and turn right (north). This street crosses Ren Min Road again, leading directly to Nanking Road where, turning right, the Peace Hotel is only one block away.

HOTEL ACCOMMODATIONS

Shanghai's hotels were originally built by Westerners in the 1930s and still recall the indulgences of that era. Although lacking in modern amenities, they are still among the most comfortable hotels in China. They maintain hand-operated elevators, rooftop dining rooms, and parquet floors. Their service is without parallel in China. Businessmen usually stay at the Peace Hotel, located directly on the waterfront and near the branch offices of the foreign trade corporations. Tourists and general delegations are also put up at the International and Shanghai Mansions. More important groups (in protocol standing) stay at the Chin Chiang, outside the central district.

□ **Peace Hotel.** Despite a faded facade, worn carpets, and a rather uninspiring lobby, the Peace Hotel (formerly Cathay Mansions) is Shanghai's most popular hostelry for foreign guests. It is located at 20 Nan Jing Lu (telephone: 211244), just at the corner of Chung Shan Road, which lines the Whangpoo River.

Rates in the 14-story, 180-room hotel range from Y28 (US$16.50) for a basic twin to Y48 (US$28.24) for a suite. In winter there is a 15% surcharge for heat. Rooms are comfortable. The dining room, which occupies the entire top floor of the hotel and commands a beautiful view of the Whangpoo River, boasts a menu that includes Chinese cuisine from five regions. Western dishes feature T-bone steaks and the best creampuffs in China.

Since Shanghai is a terminus for trans-Pacific telephone lines, international communications links are excellent. The hotel, like all others in Shanghai, has telephone, cable, and post office facilities on the premises.

Unlike taxis in Peking and Kwangchow, Shanghai's taxis do not line up at the major hotels, but they are easily summoned with the help of the main service desk in the lobby of the hotel.

□ **International Hotel.** The International (formerly the Park Hotel) is an 18-story structure that overlooks People's Park. It is situated at 170 Nanking Road (telephone: 291010). Rates are among the cheapest in Shanghai, ranging from Y22 (US$13.00) to Y38 (US$23.35). Like other hotels in the city, the restaurant (on the 12th floor) offers a good view of the surroundings and serves both Chinese and Western food. The hotel has the advantage of being located near the No. 1 Department Store—just two blocks east of the front door.

□ **Shanghai Mansions.** Foreign visitors to Shanghai are regularly taken to Shanghai Mansions at 20 North Soochow Road (telephone: 244186) for its "birds-eye view" of the city. Its ordinary guest rooms are a bit more spartan than those of its downtown counterparts, although its suites are nothing short of spectacular. Called the Broadway Mansions before 1949, it was then mainly a residential hotel used by the British. Some of the rooms still have ice boxes, grand pianos, and private balconies. Suites cost Y38 (US$23.35), with other rooms priced accordingly.

The main restaurant is on the third floor, with the top floor reserved for banquets. Some of the service staff have been with the hotel since the 1940s, and the kitchen turns out everything from bird's nest soup to lemon meringue pie.

The hotel's main asset—its picturesque location (it sits on the northern bank of Soochow Creek at the confluence of the Whangpoo) —becomes a drawback in the evening. The sonorous horns of river barges go on all night, posing a constant challenge to sleep (one of the charges against the disgraced Chiang Ch'ing was that she ordered all river traffic to cease when she slept in the city).

□ **Chin Chiang Hotel.** What this hotel lacks in convenience of location it more than makes for in elegance. Formerly a mansion used by the French as an apartment hotel, it boasts leaded-glass windows, a parquet-floored dining room, and a billiards table. In an anachronistic touch, the elevator operators wear white gloves.

The Chin Chiang is located at 189 Chang Tung Road, near Huai Hai Road, in the west-central section of Shanghai. Rooms here are in the Y30 (US$17.64) range. Communication facilities include several telex machines, located in the adjacent post office annex. The modern-style building across the courtyard was where President Nixon and Premier Chou En-lai concluded the Shanghai Communiqué on February 27, 1972.

The restaurant is on the 11th floor, at the site of the former ballroom. It serves excellent Western and Chinese food and the staff will attempt special dishes on request.

SHANGHAI CUISINE

Two characteristics dominate Shanghai's cuisine: elegant presentation and an abundance of seafood. Particularly at banquets, great attention is paid to making even the most mundane dishes appear colorful and appetizing. Carrots, turnips, beancurd, and other foods are fastidiously shaped to resemble miniature animals and flowers. Among the most famous seafood dishes is steamed freshwater crab (in season from October through December). Other items include eel (prepared in a heavy garlic sauce) and sweet-and-sour river fish. "Beggars' chicken" (small chunks cooked slowly in caked mud) is said to have originated in this area.

Unlike Peking and Kwangchow, however, Shanghai has few large restaurants that cater to foreigners. Smaller restaurants throughout the city and outdoor food stalls gladly welcome foreign visitors, but the best meals are usually found at the hotels. There is a Moslem restaurant (vegetarian) on Foochow Street and a Szechuan restaurant on An Tang Lu. Shanghai residents have a sweet tooth and among the places they favor is the Shanghai Cakes and Pastries Store on 805 Nanking Road (one block from the Peace Hotel), which prepares Western-style baked goods.

SHOPPING

The Friendship Store has shrunk from a rambling three-building affair to an efficient three-storied building. Its selection of high-quality silks still make it worth a visit. There are also some interesting pieces of jewelry on display and, if one is willing to dig for them, some attractive scrolls. It is also the only place in Shanghai where one can buy antiques, although the quantity and selection are extremely limited.

Shanghai's major section for shoppers is Nanking Road. Among its variety of shops, the visitor will find a store devoted solely to paper cuts (across the street from the department store), one specializing in *wushu* (martial arts) paraphernalia, and a large bookstore.

The Number One Department Store, at the corner of Nanking and Hsi Tang roads, near People's Park, is the largest in all of China, with merchandise arranged over four floors. It is open from 8 AM until 9PM, and includes a special section that stays open all night. The top floor has radios, gift items, and stationery. The middle two floors specialize in clothing, and the street floor has items ranging from hand luggage (the canvas bags with a picture of Shanghai stenciled on the side are a popular souvenir) to tea (prized Hangchow chrysanthemum tea is available here in bulk). Since the removal of the "gang of four" there has been a noticeable increase in consumer-oriented production in China. Featured items for Chinese now include bicycles, sewing machines, wrist watches, cameras, and colorful textiles.

About 100,000 customers a day pass through the store, which employs a staff of 1,200. The manager, who earns about $500 a year, must submit his annual plans to the Ministry of Commerce. Prices are centrally fixed and some products, such as televisions, are subsidized. Annual sales amount to Y134 million (US$78.8 million), of which 2% is profit.

Hangchow

杭
州

city across the river
Pinyin Spelling: Hangzhou ("hong-joe")

Hangchow, one of China's most famous scenic sites, is the capital of Chekiang Province, as well as its political, economic, and cultural center. Situated on the Chentang River at the southern end of the Grand Canal, it has an area of 429 sq.km. (165.6 sq.mi.) and a population of 980,000. It is also a prosperous industrial and agricultural city, with good flight connections from Peking (710 mi.), Kwangchow, Nanking, and Shanghai.

The local scenery is legendary, due largely to the beautiful West Lake (Hsi Hu). The lake was originally a shallow bay adjoining the Chentang River. Gradually, with the silting up of its outlet, it was transformed into an inland lake. Over the centuries, the lake has been repeatedly dredged. Causeways, bridges, and pavilions, subtly adorned with trees and flowers, produced a setting of such striking beauty that it became China's most popular resort.

Hangchow in History

The extension of the Grand Canal southward from the Yangtse River late in the 6th century transformed Hangchow from a sleepy fishing village into a bustling commercial center. Its continued growth was assured as the fertile lower Yangtse valley supplanted the North China Plain as the country's prime agricultural region. Between the 8th and 12th centuries, it was alternately the capital of several kingdoms and dynasties. Although devastated by the Mongol invasion of the late 13th century, Hangchow's importance did not diminish. Its function as a trade center together with the splendor of its religious monuments continued to attract merchants and visitors from all over the world (including Marco Polo).

Hangchow's political and commercial significance was dramatically curtailed in the mid-19th century as a result of the Taiping Rebellion. Much of the city was reduced to ashes, many of its most venerable religious structures were damaged or destroyed, and thousands of its inhabitants slaughtered.

115

The local guides take pride in pointing out that the city has been virtually rebuilt since 1949. Up until then, it had only a few small factories and one cotton textile mill. After the Great Leap Forward (1958), capital construction began on a massive scale. Today, old, crowded houses are overshadowed by newly-constructed apartment buildings. As the Chinese say, the city has taken on "a new look."

Economy and Culture

Industry came relatively late to Hangchow, but the pace of progress has been rapid. Before 1949, the estimated size of the workforce for the 33 small-scale and one large factory was 5,000. Today, nearly one-third of its population of 980,000 are industrial workers. The value of the city's industrial output has doubled since 1965 and is reported to have increased 24-fold since 1949. The city now boasts an iron and steel mill, machine tool factories, petrochemical and oil refining facilities, and an electronics industry. The Hsinan River Hydroelectric Power station, situated on the upper reaches of the Chengtang River, has a capacity of 650,000 kw. Power generators, light trucks, and small tractors are also manufactured in Hangchow.

The silk industry, which dates locally to the 7th century, is another economic feature of Hangchow. Natural silk fabrics, brocades, and parasols produced here are renowned for their design and quality.

The agricultural output of Hangchow is dominated by tea, which is grown by the Tea Production Brigade of the West Lake People's Commune. The commune is located near the heart of the old city of Lungching (Dragon Well), after which the tea is named.

HIGHLIGHTS FOR TRAVELERS

Areas of interest to the visitor can be divided into three parts: the city itself, local examples of modern industry and agriculture, and West Lake and its surroundings.

The city of Hangchow is endowed with few distinctive features. The crowded, narrow streets of the old section are frequently choked with traffic. However, there are also newly-constructed apartment complexes, schools, government buildings, and industrial installations, many of which face broad, tree-lined boulevards. Examples of modern developments in Hangchow often visited include:

☐ **Tu Chin Sheng Silk Brocade Factory.** Famous for its intricate brocade portraits of Chinese scenery and heroic scenes from the revolution. The mill employs 1,700 workers and uses 300 electric looms. Its annual output includes about 3 million meters of silk, including over 1,000 patterns.

☐ **West Lake People's Commune** is the home of the Lungching (Dragon Well) tea. It is now a year-around operation for the 1,300 members of the Tea Production Brigade. By careful management and intensive agricultural techniques, the tea shrubs now yield 2,100 kg. of tea leaves per hectare (1,848 lbs. per acre).

☐ **Hsinan Power Station** began generating electricity in 1960. The reservoir covers an area of 580 sq.km. (224 sq.mi.) and has a capacity of 17,800 million cu.m. (23,140 cu.yd.).

West Lake

The focal-point of a visit to Hangchow is West Lake. The lake itself has a surface area of 1,235 acres, with a 15-km. (9-mi.) shoreline. There are two dikes built to control the water flow, and the lake has four islands, the largest of which is Ku Shan ("Solitary Hill"), in the northwest.

North Shore

☐ **Solitary Hill (Ku Shan) Island.** Linked to the north shore by a bridge and to the east by the Pai Chu-yi Causeway, the island was landscaped during the T'ang Dynasty (618-907), when its first pavilion was built. Its name is misleading since the island has become a favorite stopover for visitors. Its most famous pavilion is the Autumn Moon and Calm Lake Pavilion, used as a study retreat by the K'ang Hsi Emperor of the Ch'ing Dynasty. It was so named because its appearance is most striking when cast in the clear and silvery moonlight of autumn. Other places of interest on Ku Shan include the Crane Pavilion, the Chekiang Provincial Museum (consisting of a small botanical garden and sections on physical geography, popular arts, and history), the Seal Engravers Club, and the Chekiang Library. Additions since 1949 include the Octagonal Pavilion, Quadrangular Pavilion, and the Terrace on the Lake. Cassia and maple trees grace the site.

☐ **Lotus in the Breeze at the Crooked Courtyard.** This poetic name refers to a modern pavilion and small park situated directly across from the Hangchow Hotel.

West Lake

West Shore

☐ **Su Tung-po Causeway.** This north-south causeway is the lake's largest. It has six bowed bridges (Crossing the Rainbows, Tung-po, Suppressing Dike, Viewing Hills, Locking Waves, and Reflecting Waves), and was named after the poet-governor who ruled Hangchow in the 8th century.

☐ **Viewing Fish at Flower Harbor (Hua Kang Kaun Yu).** This site is located on the southwestern end of West Lake where a small creek formerly emptied into the lake. During the Ch'ing Dynasty, a pavilion was set up on the south side and fish were stocked in an artificial pond. The area has since been enlarged to 23 hectares (55 acres) and several lotus ponds have been added. A peony garden embraces the old stream.

South Shore

☐ **Three Pools that Mirror the Moon (Santan Yinyue).** Also known as Hsia Ying Chou, this is the second largest island in the lake. It is really a series of circular embankments, creating the impression of a "lake within lakes." It is landscaped in typical Chinese style with the Nine-Bend Bridge (actually a series of right angles) linking the islets. There are many small pavilions, terraces, display rocks, and flower beds. Walkways are bounded by circular windows, each providing a different perspective for viewing the scenery.

Eastern Shore

The eastern shore of the lake has a number of parks (Chingpo, Childrens', Liu-lang-wen, and Hupin). The China Liberation Memorial is the centerpiece. A hotel for overseas Chinese is located on this side of the lake, and it is from here that boat expeditions embark. Rowboats may be rented.

Sites Surrounding West Lake

☐ **Precious Stone Hill (Pao-shu Shan).** This is the most prominent hill on the north side of the lake, with an altitude of 200 m. The hill is famous for its oddly-shaped boulders, the inspiration for an assortment of legends. There is a prehistoric cave (Chuan Ching) containing stone furniture and a seven-story pagoda originally erected in the 10th century and rebuilt in 1933.

☐ **Ko-ling Hill.** This hill, which rises just behind the Hangchow Hotel, has the Early Sun Terrace at its summit. Excellent for viewing the sunrise, it also affords the best overall view of the lake and the city of Hangchow.

☐ **Purple Cloud Cave (Tsuyun Tung).** One of the five caves on the "Mountain on Which Clouds Stay" (Chia Hsai Shan), this is a favorite place for picnics. The site is surrounded by peach trees and has a good view of the lake.

☐ **Monastery of the Souls Retreat (Lingying Su).** This Buddhist Temple was founded by the monk Wei Li in 326 AD, and is the best-known monastery in Hangchow. Its Hall of Heavenly Kings, restored in 1956, contains an 82-ft.-high Buddha.

☐ **Six Harmonies Pagoda (Liuho Ta).** This pagoda is located at the top of Yuelu Hill, on the north bank of the Chentang River. Originally built in 970 AD, it was thought that its cosmic forces would deflect the huge waves of the powerful tidal bore brought on by the full moon. It also served a practical purpose as a lighthouse for river traffic. The octagonal structure has 13 stories outside and 7 inside and was uniquely constructed with a combination of brick and wood. It is 60 m. (196 ft.) high.

☐ **Nanping Hill.** Built during the Ch'ing Dynasty, the Chin Chi Temple of Nanping Hill overlooks the south shore of West Lake. On the ceiling, it has elaborate paintings of cranes and the roof top is adorned with flying dragons. Just opposite the main entrance of the temple are the remains of the Lei Fun Pagoda, the scene of a fairy-tale romance of a scholar and a white snake.

☐ **Yen Hsia Mountain.** A number of caves are located on the sides of this hill, including the Yen Hsia Cave, the Shiu Le Cave, and the Shih Hu Cave.

HOTEL ACCOMMODATIONS

There are a number of hotels surrounding West Lake but, for the most part, only two are used by Western visitors—the Hangchow Hotel and the Lakeview Hotel, which adjoin one another on the north side of the lake. The Hangchow is a luxurious accommodation by PRC standards. It has high-ceilinged rooms, verandas, and gardens. Room rates are Y14 per twin-bedded room. The Lakeview is more modern, with nine stories and verandas for each room facing the lake. The hotels are literally steps away from some of the best scenery in Hangchow, and exploration on foot is recommended.

HANGCHOW CUISINE

Given West Lake's prominence as a resort, the chefs of the area have succeeded in elevating the level of the local cuisine to a renowned stature. A local vegetable, *shuen chai*, is one of the noted products of Hangchow. Combined in a soup with lake perch, it becomes a delicacy prized for its nutritious quality. It is said that the ancient emperors received this dish as a special tribute from the local populace. Sweet-and-sour fish, snow-white shrimps cooked with Lungching tea, and stewed duck tongues are also specialties of the region, as is the honeyed ham. Plain noodles are served with fried shrimps and eels, and there is an exotic noodle dish called "cat's ears." Other local dishes include steamed rice with lotus leaves, cassia and maize soups, and assorted pastries.

The special feature of all Hangchow dishes is the utter freshness of their ingredients. For example, stewed bamboo shoots or fried fish with spring shoots are prepared immediately after the shoots are dug from the ground and the fish caught from the pond.

For these and other dishes, the scenic Lou Wei-lou Restaurant is recommended. It is located on the Pai-chu Causeway at the southeast corner of Ku Shan Island (from the Hangchow Hotel, cross the street, walk past the Chiu Chin Tomb, and cross the Hsiling bridge to Ku Shan).

SHOPPING

Artisans maintain high standards befitting the reputation of the region, creating items of fine quality. Most famous are renderings of local scenery woven in silk. Bright colors and delicate handwork characterize Hangchow embroidery. When purchased locally, it is remarkably inexpensive (imports to the US have been limited by high duties). Chinese visitors favor the local silk umbrellas and parasols, which resemble a stalk of bamboo when closed, but reveal a painted scene when opened. Fans made in Hangchow are also renowned. Most are made of sandalwood, but other materials include ivory, turtle shell, mahogany, chicken feathers, bamboo, and coral. The overlay is either paper or silk. In keeping with local artisan traditions, even common household items produced in Hangchow carry some distinction, notably the scissors and chopsticks.

Tea lovers will appreciate the green tea (Lungching), as well as the famous chrysanthemum tea which is prized as a digestive aid. Also available for purchase are cooked hams, which are sold at the railway station of Kam Hwa (because of import regulations, these are best eaten while in China.).

EASTERN CHINA

Soochow

苏
州

plentiful water
Pinyin Spelling: Suzhou (*"soo-joe"*)

Soochow is an ancient city located on the old Imperial Canal in southern Kiangsu Province, just 86 km. (52 mi.) west of Shanghai. Noted for its scenic canals and gardens, the city has an area of 119 sq.km. (46 sq.mi.) and a population of 800,000. It is 12 miles from the banks of Lake Tai and sits astride the railway line connecting Shanghai, Wuhsi, and Nanking.

Soochow today remains unique among Chinese cities in that it has preserved much of its traditional appearance and has largely retained its economic focus on handicrafts. Although factory chimneys now far outnumber Soochow's seven pagodas, the old city is remarkably undisturbed by new construction or motor traffic—the extensive network of canals are still the city's major thoroughfares.

Soochow in History

Historical records indicate that Soochow was settled over 3,000 years ago. It rose to prominence as the capital of the Kingdom of Wu in 518 BC. At that time, the city was said to have "eight gates and eight water gates." The present name was granted in 589 AD, when work began on the Grand Canal that now runs immediately west of the city. Marco Polo visited Soochow in the 13th century and found it a "noble city and great." Its silk industry developed in the 14th century and its products are still among the most famous in China. During the Ming and Ch'ing dynasties, Soochow and its people earned repute for their subtle, graceful qualities. It was said that "In heaven there is paradise, on earth Soochow and Hangchow." (The local dialect was also highly regarded, as a popular aside had it: "Argument in Soochow is more pleasing than flattery in Kwangchow.")

Soochow was despoiled in the 19th century when the Taiping rebels briefly held the city. Treated as an adjunct to Shanghai by the Europeans, it was made a Japanese concession in the late 19th century. US and European economic interests were still prevalent throughout the first half of the 20th century.

Economy and Culture

Soochow's traditional silk industry dates back to the 14th century. Since 1949, its industry has greatly diversified, and Soochow's modern industrial output now includes mining, metallurgy, chemicals, machine-tools, electronics, and precision instruments. According to local officials, the total value of industrial output in 1974 was 28 times that of the early 1950s.

Light industry includes jade carving, woodworking, tapestries, velvets, sandalwood fans, and lacquerware.

Agricultural productivity has benefited from the widespread introduction of mechanization. Because the land is flat, the former small plots have been converted into large holdings, with rice fields now mechanically drained and irrigated. Products of the region include winter wheat, cotton, and livestock.

The city has four institutions of higher learning, including the Soochow Embroidery Institute. There are 51 middle schools and 180 primary schools, with universal education provided through the primary level.

In addition to the natural beauty of the area, the local people uphold many aspects of their district's cultural heritage, including Sukun Opera and the Pintan drama troupes which perform works with a unique local flavor.

HIGHLIGHTS FOR TRAVELERS

Gardens

It is difficult to dispute the local claim that Soochow has the most beautiful gardens in all of China. Natural ponds and waterways have been enhanced by exquisite gardens that combine traditional elements such as pavilions, temples, and rock sculptures (called rockeries) with distinctive arrangements of trees and flowers. The aim has been to create as many perspectives as possible within a confined space and to replicate in miniature scenes from nature not to be found locally.

☐ **Surging Wave Pavilion (Chang Lan).** Laid out on the site of an estate founded in the 10th century, the garden itself was completed about 1044. Following a design symbolic of the "waves of life," it has itself been destroyed several times. Its last major reconstruction came in 1873, following the Taiping Rebellion. It was re-opened to the public in 1954. A stroll through them is supposed to evoke the feeling of rambling through thickly-forested hills. Some of the names of the specific viewing places are Fish-Watching Pavilion, Pavilion for Viewing Waters, and View of the Mountain Pavilion.

☐ **Lion Garden (Shih-tze Lin).** Described in a local brochure as a "veritable labyrinth of hollow caves of spectacular shapes," the garden was first built in 1350, during the Yuan (Mongol) Dynasty. The grotesque stones come from Lake Tai. The garden has a large pond and stone boat.

☐ **Humble Administrator's Garden (Chou Cheng Yuan).** Also known as "Plain Man's Politics Garden," a Ch'in Dynasty quotation purports to explain its name: "To cultivate one's garden to meet one's daily needs, that is what is known as the politics of a plain man."

Water is the main attraction of the site, covering three-fifths of the garden. Originally constructed during the Ming Dynasty, the East Garden was completely restored after 1949 (older portions are easily identified—the lines on old buildings are more subtle and greater attention was paid to detail in decorations). Bridges zig-zag at right angles across the ponds. Places of interest include the Hall of Distant

Fragrance, Small Flying-Rainbow Bridge, Pavilion of Fragrant Snow and Azure Clouds, and Pavilion of Expecting Frost.

☐ **Tarrying Garden (Liu Yuan).** Laid out under the Ming Dynasty, this garden is about a half-mile northwest of town. Originally a large country villa, it was rebuilt as a public garden and took its present name in 1876. The east section features halls and corridors decorated with calligraphy. Ponds and covered promenades mark the central section. The western section is known for its wooded landscapes.

☐ **Garden of Harmony (Yi Yuan).** The most "natural" of the many gardens around Soochow, this site features pools with colored pebbles and innumerable flower beds. The garden is noted for four characteristics: stones from the lake, tablets above the entrances, pine trees, and animals.

☐ **Tiger Hill (Huchiu).** This artificial hill is located two miles northwest of the main city, and is a "must" on the itinerary. It reaches a height of 36 m. and includes all of the traditional elements considered essential to the "perfect" hill: stones, rocks, plants, trees, pagodas, waterfalls, and a multitude of legends.

The hill was built over 2,500 years ago (during the Spring and Autumn period) by the King of Wu (490 BC) as the tomb for his father. Legend has it that a tiger guards his tomb (hence the name). The Yunyan Pagoda at the summit was built in 961 AD. Over the centuries it began to tilt, but it has lately been reinforced with concrete and steel bars.

Among the noted sights on the hill are Han Han Spring, which supposedly could be diverted to flood secret passages to keep out intruders. A huge flat stone known as the Stone of a Thousand Men was so named because the stains on the surface of the stone were believed to be the blood of the thousand workers who built the tomb. There is also a Sword Testing Stone (the Chinese, as many other cultures, have their own version of the King Arthur Legend), where archeologists have found some clues about the original tomb.

Grand Canal

The Grand Canal is located immediately west of the city and is the largest man-made waterway in the world. Originally constructed to bear tribute rice from the Yangtse Plain north to Peking, portions of it are still active. The segment adjacent to Soochow is heavily traversed by long lines of cargo barges carrying agricultural products and raw materials from commune fields to urban processing plants or warehouses. The canal's embankments are well-constructed masonry structures with towpaths still in use. The width of the canal averages 100 ft. but narrows to about 30 ft. at the numerous picturesque stone bridges that arch gracefully above it. Depths average 7-10 ft., adequate for small river craft.

Silk Mills

☐ **'East is Red' Silk Weaving Mill.** Growing from a small backyard workshop to a major facility with 730 pieces of equipment, the mill's 2,000 workers turn out 250 varieties of fabric.

☐ **Soochow Silk Printing Mill.** The factory was founded in 1958 and is almost completely mechanized. It produces nearly a thousand patterns of pure silk, rayon, and other fibers. Many of its products are made specifically for export.

☐ **Tungshan Tungting Commune.** This commune has a diversified economy of grain, fruit, fish, and silk, and is especially known for its tangerines and shrimp (gathered from Lake Tai).

HOTEL ACCOMMODATIONS

Visitors to Soochow will find themselves comfortably situated in the Soochow Grand Hotel, located on "Friendship Road." Near to the Chang Lang Pavilion and Garden, the hotel is set among farmhouses in a charming old section of the city. Rooms are old-fashioned with comfortable furnishings and old-style bathrooms. Although not air-conditioned, the heat of the summer is moderated by its thick concrete construction.

LOCAL CUISINE

Soochow has a well-earned reputation for dining. The city's restaurants—usually small and simply furnished—have traditionally attracted patrons from as far away as Nanking and Shanghai. The restaurants do an especially brisk business during the city's numerous food festivals, the most popular ones coinciding with changes in season. Fish and rice, the two items that dominate the region's food output, are featured.

One of the most esteemed festivals is the crab feast, which occurs in early autumn. Area fishermen congregate at a small shallow lake 5 mi. to the northeast of Soochow. There, armed with bamboo traps, they snare crabs as they emerge from the crevices where they have just laid eggs. The resulting dish is called "Ta-cha-hsieh." Other items known around Soochow are candies, pickled ducks, and tea.

SHOPPING

Handicraft fanciers will also enjoy Soochow, which is known for its embroidery, sandalwood fans, jade carvings, wrought gems, and, of course, Soochow silks. Selections are available at the Friendship Store, across from the "Wonderful Lookout" on Kuan-ch'ien Street, or at the department store, located on Ren Min Road just across the street from the Pleasure Garden. Both are within two and a half miles from the hotel.

EASTERN CHINA

Wuhsi

without tin

Pinyin Spelling: Wuxi ("woo-shee")

Wuhsi (also spelled Wushi), in Kiangsu Province, is an industrial and resort city on the north bank of Lake Tai (Taihu), one of China's five largest lakes. Important as a transportation junction, Wuhsi is situated astride the Grand Canal, and along the Nanking-Shanghai railway line, 145 km. (87 mi.) west of Shanghai. Wuhsi has an area of 204 sq.km. (78.7 sq.mi.) and a population of 650,000. The original name of the city, Yu Hsi ("with tin"), referred to local tin mines first worked in the Chou Dynasty. When the tin was depleted during the Han Dynasty, the name was changed to "Wuhsi" ("without tin").

Wuhsi in History

Wuhsi's long history dates back some 3,000 years to the Shang and Chou periods, when scattered settlements existed in the area. The city was formally founded during the Han Dynasty when it became the capital of a feudal state in the region. Yet, few details appear in later dynastic histories and Wuhsi remained for the most part a small country town. This image did not begin to change until the 1930s, when the town began rapidly to expand its industry, the keystone of which were 45 silk filature factories. Wuhsi also gained some importance as a transport center, transshipping manufactured goods and silks by water to Shanghai. Its greatest period of expansion, however, came after 1949.

Economy and Culture

Wuhsi has long been associated with silk production, an activity that had its origins in the area some 1,500 years ago. Silk-reeling and weaving workshops were set up in the mid-19th century, but the industry remained relatively stagnant during the first decades of this century. After the founding of the PRC in 1949, the silk filature factories (which separate silk fibers from the cocoons and wind them onto spools) were rebuilt, and related activities such as silk weaving, dying, and printing were started up.

Today, the city is also known for high-technology products such as diesel engines, air compressors, electric cables, boilers, precision instruments, machine tools, and electronics parts. In total there are 470 factories in Wuhsi employing some 249,000 skilled workers. Light industry includes the production of bicycles, enamelware, glassware, and the famous Huishan Pottery Works. The city also produces concrete boats for use on the region's numerous small canals (these boats are actually lighter than wooden craft and have greater maneuverability and speed; moreover, they require less upkeep).

Wuhsi is surrounded by rich agricultural land capable of yielding three rice crops a year. Pig breeding and fishing are also important in the Lake Tai area.

The city has 150 primary and middle schools and one university; enrollment at all levels is approximately 140,000 students. In addition, some of the factories have their own part-time technical schools for training workers. Wuhsi also has 12 hospitals and a prominent historical library.

HIGHLIGHTS FOR TRAVELERS

☐ **Hsihui Park.** Located on the western outskirts of Wuhsi, this park encompasses the neighboring Hui hills, including "Tin Hill." Two famous sights are its temples and the Chi Chang Garden ("Garden for Ease of Mind"), all dating back to the Ming Dynasty. The garden at the foot of the hill was rebuilt recently as an exact replica of the 16th-century original. The temple on top of Hui Hill was built in 420 AD and affords a broad view of the surrounding region. Several pavilions and tea houses are scattered throughout the park. On hot summer days, the exquisitely decorated stone-slab chairs are always cool to the touch.

□ **Huishan Clay Figure Workshop.** Local artisans of the Ming era were the first to discover the qualities of Hui Mountain clay. Excellent for molding, it also dries to a remarkable hardness and is thus excellent for firing. The local pottery factory underwent a modern revival in 1954 and now employs some 600 persons, about 60% female. Most of the figures now made reflect contemporary literary and political themes. More than one-third of the output is exported. The factory has a small retail outlet for visitors.

□ **Wuhsi Number One Silk Filature Factory.** Another common spot on the visitor's itinerary is the Number One Silk Filature Factory. The vast majority of its workers are women. The mill dates from 1933 and prior to 1949 had an average annual production of 40 tons of raw silk. The present output is well over eight-times that amount, and the newly installed semi-automatic machines enable a worker to tend 60 threads of silk at a time.

Grand Canal

Wuhsi sits astride the Grand Canal and is among the last major stops on the way to Hangchow from Peking. The Canal is excluded from most itineraries, possibly because it still reflects aspects of "old" China—much canal traffic is still manually propelled. The main canal dates from 605 AD, when it connected the Yellow River in the north (at Loyang) with the Yangtse in the south. By 610, the entire canal route from Peking to Hangchow was opened. Later, in the Yuan (Mongol) Dynasty, the northern segment of the canal was redredged and, over the centuries, it has remained a basic means of supplying the capital city and its border armies with food from the south. The main bridge over the canal is a short distance from the central square of the city.

Lake Tai

Lake Tai (Tai Hu) has an area of some 2,240 sq.km. (864 sq.mi.) and includes about 100 islands. Many of its sights may be visited by boat in the course of a morning or afternoon excursion.

☐ **Workers Sanitorium.** Although several of these are located around the lake, most visitors tour the facility on Chungtu Island. It comprises three compounds with over 300 beds and commands a superb view of the lake and surrounding area. Both traditional Chinese medicine (acupuncture, moxibustion) and Western medicine are used to help patients, as well as physiotherapy and physical training programs.

☐ **Turtle Head Island (Yuantou Tsu).** This small, pleasant island is situated on the south shore of the lake. The island forms the head of a turtle, hence its name. There are several arched bridges, pavilions, and walkways, but the emphasis is on the natural scenery, especially the lake itself with its barges and fleets of sailing vessels. On the "head" of the turtle stands a small lighthouse, near which is a stone inscribed with the island's name.

☐ **Three Hills in Lake Tai.** The main peak has a restaurant that overlooks the lake and Turtle Head Island. Pears and apples, the source of considerable local pride, are featured.

☐ **Li Garden (Liyuan).** One of three famous gardens in Wuhsi, Li Garden lies south of the city on Lake Li, a smaller body that feeds into Lake Tai. The public garden reflects classic Chinese design, with grotesque rockeries, bow bridges, pavilions, walkways built on dikes that cross the lake, and varieties of flora. There is a miniature five-story pagoda at the mid-lake pavilion. It is reached via a covered promenade with wooden walls perforated by 89 flower-shaped windows. Ancient legend has it that the garden was founded by a local king who courted a princess there.

HOTEL ACCOMODATIONS

☐ **Taihu Hotel.** This is a modern structure with a magnificent view of the lake. It is a two-story building with spacious, high-ceilinged rooms and small, screened windows that overlook the lake. Hotel services include a good restaurant, retail shop, and post and telephone facilities. Room rates are Y9 (US$5.10) per day. In front of the hotel is a garden with a duck pond. Recreational equipment is available to guests. About four miles from the hotel are a cluster of mulberry farms with a small village at its core. A walk to this area affords an excellent view of rural China. The local people are open and receptive, and school children are likely to greet visitors with a warm "Hello!"

REGIONAL CUISINE

It is probably more difficult in Wuhsi than in most cities in China to "drop in" on a local restaurant. The hotel dining room generally serves the standard fare (although excellently prepared). Fish dishes, of course, are quite popular, with shrimp, crab, and crisp-fried eel heading the list. Spareribs are another good local dish, prepared with a bean-curd sauce.

SHOPPING

Shoppers will be attracted by the fine regional handicrafts, including pottery figurines, briar pipes, and linen embroideries. Silk products, the local specialty, range from finely woven "paintings" to fabrics suitable for dresses. The shop at the Taihu Hotel store features a selection of semi-precious stones. Wuhsi also has a rarely frequented antiques store that has been known to feature items long since "bought up" in the larger cities.

EASTERN CHINA

Nanking

southern capital
Pinyin Spelling: Nanjing ("nan-jing")

Nanking is situated amidst one of China's most splendid natural settings. It sits in a basin formed by the Yangtse River on the north and the Tsechin (purple) Mountains on the other sides. The image suggested to ancient writers was one of "dragon curling and tiger crouching." The city has several times served as the capital of China. Today, it is the capital of Kiangsu Province. Located about 300 km. (186 mi.) up river from Shanghai, it has an area of 778.6 sq. km. (300 sq. mi.), with a population of 2.5 million.

After its natural scenery, the dominant feature of Nanking is the Yangtse River Bridge. Built in 1968, it serves as a key link in the country's north-south transportation system, with Peking lying 1,157 km.

(719 mi.) by rail to the north and Kwangchow 2,127 km. (1,322 mi.) to the south.

Nanking's climate is marked by intense dry heat during the summer months—the origin of its reputation as one of the "five furnaces of the Yangtse." The city remains temperate throughout the remainder of the year, with a rainy season in late spring.

Nanking in History

Although archeological relics indicate the area was first settled some 6,000 years ago, the city of Nanking itself dates from the 8th century BC. Its importance grew when it became the capital of the Six Dynasties Period (229-589 AD). Records show that it was an active river port, sustained a variety of crops, and had established China's first iron foundries (working iron found in the nearby mountains).

Nanking served as a capital again during the Southern T'ang period (937-75) when, in addition to being a center of commerce, it also had a notable reputation for its intellectual, cultural, and artistic achievements. Buddhism flourished here and it was the home of the poetic master Li Po.

Nanking owes its present character and dimensions largely to the founders of the Ming Dynasty, who built their first capital there. To ensure the city's growth, the emperor ordered 20,000 wealthy families to move there and bestowed honors on those who underwrote new construction and economic expansion. This policy lasted for only one generation, as the succeeding Ming emperor moved the capital to Peking.

As an "adjunct capital," Nanking retained importance. Under the succeeding Ch'ing Dynasty, the development of the city advanced on many levels. Its silk and cotton industries achieved wide repute. *The Scholars*, perhaps the most noteworthy work of fiction from this period (and still widely read in the PRC), is set in Nanking and vividly re-creates its 18th-century society.

The Opium War (1842) was formally terminated with the signing of the Treaty of Nanking (opening up five treaty ports to Westerners) aboard a British gun boat in the city's harbor. In 1911, the town took part in the revolution that established the Republic of China. Afterwards, delegates of the then 17 provinces of China met in Nanking to elect Sun Yat-sen as president of the Republic. Within a year, however, China's capital was once again moved to Peking. During the civil war period, Nanking was used as a capital by the Kuomintang.

Role in the Chinese Revolution. PRC historians consider the rebellions of the 18th and 19th centuries to be antecedents of their own revolutionary struggles in the 1920s, '30s, and '40s. They cite Nanking's capture during the Taiping Rebellion in 1853 as a key event in that process. The Taipings established their own government there. Palaces were built and new coins were struck. Their rule lasted for 11 years (until 1864), whereupon Chinese armies (led by the British General "Chinese" Gordon) recaptured the city, inflicting considerable damage. During the early part of the 20th century, it was an important political and strategic area controlled by the Kuomintang. PRC narratives point to repeated uprisings, strikes, boycotts, and demonstrations of this period—mounted against the prevailing conditions of hunger, civil war, and persecution. Thousands of Nanking's citizens are said to have given their lives to the revolutionary cause.

In April 1949, the Eighth Route Army—whose forces had swelled to over a million—captured Nanking. The campaign was led personally by Mao Tse-tung. In a poem, Mao wrote: "The city, a tiger crouching, a dragon curling, outshines its ancient glories; in heroic triumph, heaven and earth have been overturned."

Economy and Culture

Since 1950, Nanking's industrial sector has been greatly expanded. There are now 1,500 industrial and mining enterprises employing 300,000 workers (before the revolution, the work force was estimated at only 10,000). Industry in Nanking includes coal mining, metallurgy, petroleum refining, machine-tool manufacturing, and auto and shipbuilding enterprises. The city also manufactures chemical equipment, telecommunication instruments, optical devices, and synthetic fibers. Nanking still serves as an important Yangtse River port.

There are 63 agricultural communes distributed among the five suburban districts and two counties under Nanking's administration. Together, these units farm 110,000 hectares (271,810 acres) of land producing grain, tea, vegetables, apples, cherries, and watermelons. Today's per-hectare grain yield of 7,100 kg. (15,656 lbs.) is 3.5 times greater than that of the early 1950s. Nanking is also proud of its afforestation programs—over 28 million trees have been planted since 1949.

There has been a correspondingly rapid growth in the city's cultural, educational, and medical facilities. Nanking now has 14 institutions of higher learning, 340 middle schools, and over 1,500 primary schools, with a combined student population of about 550,000. The most famous learning institution is Nanking University, founded in 1902. It has 12 departments with 41 specialties and, in 1976, managed three small factories and a farm. The Nanking Normal School, sometimes visited by foreigners, trains teachers.

There are some 18,000 medical workers in the Nanking area, serving in 107 hospitals and 740 public health institutions. Over 10,000 hospital beds are available.

Yangtse River Bridge, Nanking

HIGHLIGHTS FOR TRAVELERS

☐ **Yangtse River Bridge.** It is hard to overstate the symbolic importance of the Yangtse River Bridge and the pride which all Chinese take in it. Until its completion in 1968, there was no direct overland link between the important lower Yangtse Valley (encompassing Nanking and Shanghai) and Peking. But even more significant perhaps is the bridge's psychological importance: the 70-ft. depths of swirling, silt-laden waters—covering a bedrock floor—had proved too much of a challenge to Western and Soviet engineers. Relying completely on their own efforts, the Chinese undertook the building of the bridge in 1960. An average of 7,000 workers were engaged daily in its construction. On October 1, 1968, the "Mao Tse-tung Locomotive" crossed the span, marking its completion. The bridge is 1,577 m. (5,171 ft.) long between bridge heads. It has two levels, with a wide roadway on the upper level and a dual-track railway on the lower.

☐ **Sun Yat-sen Mausoleum.** Sun Yat-sen, the leader of the 1911 Revolution that overthrew the old dynastic system, founded the first national government in Nanking in 1912. Although a native of Kwangchow, Sun expressed a desire to be interred here and, upon his death in 1925, construction of this imposing monument was begun. The mausoleum is situated on the southern slopes of the Tsechin Mountains in the city's eastern suburbs. The grounds cover 80,000 sq.m. (95,680 sq.yd. or 20 acres), and the memorial hall itself is approached by climbing 392 steps made of Soochow granite.

Within the domed circular hall is a white statue of Sun. An exhibition includes replicas of his will and an inscription of his Three Principles for leading China's people into a new age: "nationalism, democracy, and livelihood." The vault itself contains his coffin (the ashes were moved there from Peking in 1929 when the monument was completed) and is surmounted by a reclining statue of Sun.

☐ **Ling Ku Park.** This park is regarded by local residents as one of the "famous 40 scenic spots" of Nanking, and is located just south of the Mausoleum of Sun Yat-sen, at the foothills of the Tsechin Mountains. The park has several well-kept gardens and is particularly favored in summer for its dense pine forest. The main feature is the Wu Liang Temple, built in 1381 but rebuilt several times since. The park also has a 61 m. (200 ft.) pagoda.

☐ **Kiangsu Provincial Museum.** On the eastern outskirts of the city, just inside the Sun Yat-sen (Chung Shan Men) Gate, is the Kiangsu Provincial Museum, with a collection spanning 5,000 years of Chinese history. There are six exhibition rooms displaying prehistoric artifacts; Shang Dynasty pottery, bronzes, jewelry, and tortoise shells; iron agricultural tools; printed works; handicrafts from the Ming and Ch'ing Dynasties; furniture; and a display on the Taiping Rebellion.

☐ **Tsechin Mountain Observatory.** The observatory, the third largest in China (after Peking and Shanghai), was begun in 1934. A staff of 250 is engaged in research under auspices of the Chinese Academy of Sciences. The main interest for visitors is the museum of astronomy. The Chinese were the first civilization to develop this science. On display is a replica of the original armillary sphere (a set of circles and rings showing the relative position of heavenly bodies), invented over 1,800 years ago. There is also an ancient celestial globe and a device used to detect movement of the stars.

☐ **Ming Tomb.** T'ai Tzu (1327-98), founder of the Ming Dynasty, was buried in Nanking in a magnificent tomb, constructed in 1381.

The Taiping Rebellion laid the tomb to waste and today there remains only a stone gate and courtyard. The primary feature is a sacred path leading to the site, which is lined with 12 pairs of stone animals.

☐ **Hsuan Wu Lake.** Also known as Yuan Wu Lake, it is located in People's Park just outside the city's Hsuan Wu Gate. The park is roughly 15 km. (9.3 mi.) in circumference and was formerly a private imperial preserve. It was first opened to the public in 1911 but was not restored to its present condition until the early 1950s. The lake contains five islets, linked by embankments and classic bowed bridges (Huang Island has a pagoda). The lake itself is noted for its fish and magnificent lotus blossoms in summer. Amenities include a zoo, children's playground, skating rink, and open-air theater.

☐ **Mo Chou Lake.** Another "Chingling scenic spot," (Chingling is the former name of Nanking), the area was first developed in the 5th century AD as a garden retreat for a female member of the royal household. The Pavilion of Victory at Chess survives from the Ming Dynasty, although most of the park's attractions date from the 1950s. New additions include the Lotus Water Terrace, the cherry-apple garden, and an open-air theater. Guides will also point out the collections of fine redwood furniture and some famous examples of calligraphy and painting.

☐ **T'ang Shan Hot Springs.** For those with ample time, an excursion to the neighboring T'ang Mountains (40 km.—24.8 mi.) is recommended. The hot springs here have curative waters that maintain a constant temperature of 40° C (104° F) and contain potassium, sulphur, and calcium. Long immersions are said to be an aid to skin ailments.

☐ **Yu Hua Tsai Park.** Formerly known as Yu Hua T'ai Gardens, legend dates its origins to the 6th century AD when a Buddhist priest so impressed heaven with his sermonizing that the skies opened and flowers fell like rain. The more prosaic will note that it is the colorful, finely-grained pebbles of the area that lend it its rainbow-like hues.

Today, the park serves as a memorial to over 100,000 persons said to have been executed in Nanking during its 22 years of Nationalist rule. Thus, the site is also known as Martyrs' Park.

WALKING TOURS

Nanking does not lend itself to quick exploration on foot. The main business district, parks, and historic sites are quite a distance from the hotel. Most visitors are content to walk along the broad boulevard outside the hotel grounds which includes many buildings erected during the era of Western presence in Nanking.

☐ **Shan Hsi Lu Square** (1 hour). Shan Hsi Lu Square can be reached in a straight 15-minute walk after turning right from the hotel gate. Although some distance from downtown, this market area is always quite busy. A department store is located on the southeast corner of the square and a neighborhood medical clinic just to the southwest (on the north side of Hunan Road). There are also some "store front" factories. Vendors— ranging from shoe repairers to vegetable sellers —line the street around the square itself.

☐ **Hsuan Wu Park; Drum Tower** (2 hours). Hsuan Wu Park is too vast to explore in a short time, but a two-hour roundtrip walk will enable one to explore highlights of the park. Turn right outside the hotel gate. At Shan Hsi Lu Square bear left, heading directly east along Hunan Road. Hunan Road ends at Taching Road. Turn left and, after a short block, right at the first intersection. This leads directly to the main entrance of the park.

HOTEL ACCOMMODATIONS

☐ **Nanking Hotel.** The Nanking Hotel is known for its tranquil setting. Surrounded by gardens and a high wall (with a soldier standing guard), it is located on Sun Yat-sen Boulevard, a street lined with plane trees brought from France in the 1930s. Even the large political billboard located directly across from the front entrance does not detract from the peacefulness of the setting.

Although some rooms are air-conditioned, they are not particularly luxurious or cheerful by Western standards. The rates are Y10 per day (US$6.00). The kitchen is excellent—serving everything from regional specialties to what has become renowned as the best chocolate soufflé in China (orders should be placed well in advance).

The main disadvantage of the hotel is its relatively remote location—about an hour's walk from the central shopping district. A new hotel should be completed by early 1979.

NANKING CUISINE

Each region of China boasts its local delicacies, and Nanking is no exception. Autumn is the season for plump lake crabs. Other specialties are pickled vegetables, ducks (particularly their kidneys), and fish. Cherries, watermelon, and other fresh fruits are in abundance. The tea from the nearby hills has renowned aroma and flavor.

SHOPPING

The shopper will find the craftsmen of Nanking skilled at making reproductions of old relics such as tomb figurines. Chinese tourists often collect pebbles from the Yu Hua Terrace (Martyrs' Park), which will reflect an array of colors when placed in water.

EASTERN CHINA

Tsingtao

green island
Pinyin Spelling: Qingdao ("tzing-dow")

Tsingtao, a seaside resort and busy seaport, is situated on the southern coast of the Shantung Peninsula overlooking the Yellow Sea. The city, some 250 miles southeast of Peking, with a population of 1.5 million, is also the most important industrial town in Shantung Province. Surrounded on three sides by the sea, with Mt. Laoshan as the backdrop, Tsingtao's red-tiled roofs and verdant foliage complement its picturesque setting.

The city was a small fishing village until the Germans "selected" it as a port in 1898 and forced a treaty on China's imperial government. Within a decade, the Germans threw up a modern city with deep-water harbor, business district, and—characteristically for areas under foreign control—a separate area for Chinese residents. With 2,000 soldiers stationed in the city, the Germans mined the coal in the area to fuel their ships. During World War I, Japan took over rights to the city. It was not until 1922 that the Chinese regained control of Tsingtao.

Before 1949, the city's economy relied on trade, silk weaving, essential oils, and a brewery (perhaps the only positive reminder of the German occupation is the excellent beer, still served in its familiar green bottles).

Since the founding of the PRC, Tsingtao's industrial output has increased more than ten-fold and includes textiles, textile machinery, machine tools, and a diesel locomotive plant. Sites of interest to the visitor now include the port itself, fine bathing beaches (the cool current keeps the city comfortable during the hot summer months), an aquarium, and Lu Hsun Park.

Tsinan

Tsinan (Jinan), the capital of Shantung Province, is known as the "City of Springs," having over 100 bubbling hot springs. It is an industrial city on the Peking-Shanghai railway, some 350 km. (217 mi.) south of Peking. Tsinan's population is 1,200,000.

The major industries in Tsinan include metallurgy, machine-building, chemicals, and textiles. Agricultural products include wheat, corn, cotton, tobacco, and a good variety of fruits (peaches, pears, grapes, and dates). It also is known for its peanuts. There is a university serving the region, several medical schools, and a large industrial exhibition hall.

Tsinan has some historical sites of interest (a pagoda, "Buddha Cliff," and a T'ang Dynasty temple), but its chief attractions are the hot springs that appear all over the city. The four main springs have parks built around them and sport colorful names: Paotu (Gushing from the Ground); Heihu (Black Tiger); Wulungtan (Five Dragon Pool); and Shentzu (Pearls). These streams find their way into Taming Lake, which has an area of 460,000 sq. m. and occupies about one-fourth of the town's total area. It provides an idyllic setting, with water lillies and numerous gardens.

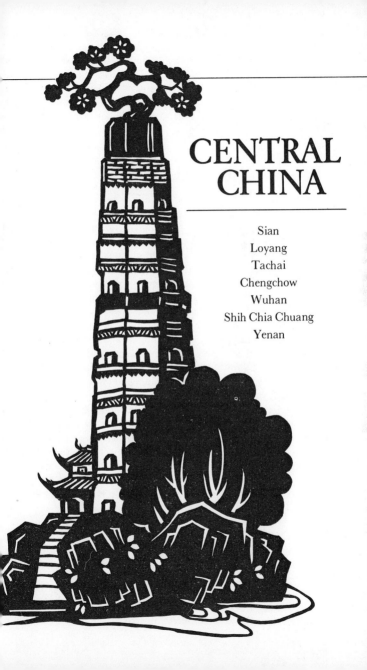

CENTRAL CHINA

Sian
Loyang
Tachai
Chengchow
Wuhan
Shih Chia Chuang
Yenan

Sian

western peace
Pinyin spelling: Xi'an ("shee-ahn")

Of all cities on the China itinerary, Sian's history most vividly exemplifies the extraordinary continuity of Chinese civilization. Once the largest city in the world and a paradigm of imperial splendor, Sian served as the capital of 11 dynasties. It was an active link in the major trade routes between China and the commercial enclaves of Central Asia and Europe during the 7th and 8th centuries. Today, Sian is a model example of the PRC government's concerted efforts to create new inland centers of industry to counterbalance the traditional dominance of the large east coast cities.

Sian, now the capital of Shensi Province, is about as far west in China as most travelers get. It is situated at the western end of a roughly equilateral triangle connecting Peking and Shanghai. It lies about 900 km. (559 mi.) southwest of Peking by air; by rail, the trip covers 1,165 km. (724 mi.), consuming 24 hours. The distance to Shanghai is 1,511 km. (938 mi.).

To the north of this city of 1,900,000 people lie the rugged Western Hills, dotted with ancient tombs. The Wei River forms a natural boundary on the north and the entire area lies in a fertile basin suitable for cotton and coarse grain. Architecturally, modern Sian is rather undistinguished, with low buildings and wide streets typical of the PRC's urban restorations. In summer, the heat shimmers off the pavement; in winter, the climate is dry and cold.

Sian in History

Remains of a neolithic village in nearby Pan P'o indicate that the area was inhabited at least 8,000 years ago. Sian was effectively the capital of China as long ago as the 11th century BC with the founding of the Western Chou Dynasty (ca. 1030 BC). It became China's first true capital in 212 BC, presiding over the unified domain of Emperor Ch'in Shih-huang. Then known as Ch'ang An, the city flourished politically, culturally, and commercially. In 129 BC, it was linked by

140

water to other regions of China by means of a canal that fed into the Wei River.

Sian subsequently served as a capital during the Sui and T'ang eras, during which time its area was considerably enlarged. The population then numbered about 1 million people. Its strategic location along Asian trade routes brought frequent contacts with foreigners (evidence of these contacts is provided in tomb figurines that depict bearded horsemen, an anomalous combination in China up to that time). Scattered remains of its palaces, imperial compound, city walls, and tombs of the T'ang emperors are still evident.

Following the demise of the T'ang Dynasty at the start of the 10th century, Sian entered a decline and, despite periods of revival, never regained its prior eminence. With the establishment of the Ming Dynasty (1368), a new palace was added to house the emperor's son. The Manchus occupied the town during the Ch'ing Dynasty, but its diminished stature by that point is indicated by the fact that 19th-century Sian was only one-sixth the size of the T'ang Dynasty capital eight centuries before.

Before the advent of modern communication links, Sian remained rather isolated. This condition began to change after 1930 with the completion of a rail spur that linked Sian to Chengchow and cities to the west and north.

In 1936, Chiang Kai-shek visited the nearby hot springs to rest from his campaign against the Communists and warlords. In an event later known as the "Sian Incident," Chiang was kidnapped by a local warlord who sought to compel Chiang to negotiate peace with the Communists and join in a united front against the Japanese. Chou En-lai was dispatched to Sian to negotiate on behalf of the Communisits and, despite Chiang's attempt to escape, a temporary agreement was effected.

The most dramatic changes in Sian have come about since 1949 The city has developed into the textile center of the northwest. Many other new industries (fertilizers, chemicals) have been introduced. Its great wide streets are now paved. New buildings, department stores, sports grounds, and a modern transportation system have contributed to its transformation.

Economy and Culture

When briefing visitors, local officials will often point out that Sian is now a city that "walks on two legs." That is, the industrial and agricultural sectors function in ways that are mutually supportive. More-

Peasant Painters, Huhsien County

over, both account for a roughly equal contribution to the local economy. Traditionally, agriculture had predominated. The area is ideal for growing wheat and cotton, crops which have particularly benefited from mass programs to extend irrigation systems in the area. Corn is also produced, as are various fruits and vegetables.

Industrialization did not come to Sian until the 1950s, but has since taken root dramatically. Local enterprises produce textiles, fertilizers, plastics, boilers, machine tools, and electrical motors, with many products applied to local agricultural use Sian artisans produce shell and feather paintings and carved lacquerware items. An enamelware factory turns out everything from ash trays to wash basins.

Sian is the site of 11 of Shensi's 15 universities and research institutions, together employing a staff of about 20,000. This region of China has its own theatrical and operatic traditions which continue to thrive. Huhsien, a county west of Sian, has become world-famous for its peasant painters, a tradition begun in the late 1950s. Exhibitions of their work have toured the UK, France, Canada, and, in 1978, the US.

HIGHLIGHTS FOR TRAVELERS

The chief interest in Sian is its archeological legacy. There are myriad tombs, temples, ruins, and other sites of interest in the area, although visitors generally have enough time to see but a few.

☐ **Shensi Provincial Museum.** Housed in a former Confucian temple in the southern district of the city, this museum boasts one of the richest collections of ancient artifacts in all of China. Three main buildings and three annexes have been remodeled twice in the last five years and can accommodate as many as 4,000 separate exhibits. Notable objects include sandstone and granite animal figures, T'ang Dynasty stone friezes, bronzes, neolithic pottery, and jewelry. Detailed captions (in English) provide helpful descriptions of the items.

The museum's centerpiece is its "forest of steles," a collection of 1,095 stone tablets (some carved by emperors) on which ancient texts —including the Confucian classics—were etched, resulting in a magnificent array of classical calligraphy. The museum also houses a replica of an old Buddhist temple. Recently, it has displayed examples of the life-sized sculptures of horses and riders discovered in 1976 in the tomb of Ch'in Shih-huang (reigned 212-206 BC).

☐ **Bell Tower.** As Sian has grown and changed contours over the centuries, its Bell Tower, built in the 15th century, has been moved repeatedly so as always to display the time at the center of town. The 69-foot-high structure has a square brick foundation and is surmounted by a two-story wooden tower adorned by gracefully arched roofs. The first floor is now used as a briefing room (it held prisoners during the civil war). In the interest of utility, the original 15th-century iron bell has been replaced by a garish lamp. The second-floor veranda provides an excellent view of the city, including the Drum Tower just one block to the west.

☐ **Small Wild Goose Pagoda.** This 140-foot-high pagoda was first built in 706 AD and soon afterwards destroyed by the ravages of war. It was again damaged during a major 16th-century earthquake. Still bearing its scars, the frail structure has remained closed to visitors. A pleasant garden surrounds the pagoda, with a stunning collection of poppies. There are no wild geese in evidence, however, and the origins of the pagoda's name remain obscure.

☐ **Big Wild Goose Pagoda.** Originally built as a Buddhist retreat (7th century), it is said to have been first used to translate Buddhist texts (brought from India) into Chinese. Like many similar struc-

Sian's Drum Tower

tures, it was destroyed and rebuilt several times during the ensuing centuries. The 240-foot, seven-story pagoda that survives dates from 1580.

The pagoda was restored in the early 1950s and today it is a popular place to get an overview of the city and the surrounding countryside. Some idea of the size and importance of the ancient city of Sian may be gained from noting that although the pagoda today stands south of the edge of the city, during T'ang times it was well within the city walls.

☐ **Pan P'o Village.** About 10 km. (6 mi.) east of Sian, on a site overlooking the Chan River, is a neolithic site of the Yang-Shao culture (ca. 6000 BC). It was discovered accidentally in 1953 when the foundations for a factory were being laid. Subsequent digging revealed a village of 45 houses, with remarkably preserved examples of stone-age pottery (bearing playful designs), tools, and animal bones. The objects are displayed in a large exhibition hall at the entrance to the grounds.

The site of the village itself has been protected through the construction of a freestanding building that covers the entire site. The visitor views the excavation from a wooden walkway that produces the uncanny sensation of footsteps echoing through 8,000 years of history. Original foundations are visible, along with reconstructed replicas of the houses.

☐ **Sian Hot Springs.** On a typical morning outing, visitors are driven some 24 km. (15 mi.) to the east of Sian for a quick tour and/or a quick bath, then on to the nearby tomb of Emperor Ch'in Shihhuang, and back to the hotel in time for lunch.

Records reveal that the springs were used by royal families as early as the 8th century BC, when a palace was built on the site. In the 10th century AD, it served as a monastery for the Taoist community, but was later reopened to the general public. The Hot Springs were the site of the Sian Incident. A steep trail leads up to a pavilion overlooking the valley where Chiang Kai-shek was recaptured while trying to escape.

The area has been rebuilt since 1949 as a resort for the general public. The central garden surrounds a large pond with water lillies. There are several tea houses and a series of low-slung buildings equipped with individual baths. Visitors are usually encouraged to "briefly" sample the 40° C (104° F) waters. The place attracts visitors from all over China.

☐ **Tumulus of Ch'in Shih-huang Ti.** The Emperor Ch'in Shih-huang was the founder of the Ch'in Dynasty. Despite evidence of extreme harshness, he is much admired in China today for his success in unifying the country, first militarily and then culturally and economically. A consummate pragmatist, he decreed that all carts be made the same width so that they could travel over standardized trails and produce uniform grooves on muddy roadways. Two large stone steles mark the path through the wheat fields to the tomb's summit. Today, the hill is covered with pomegranate trees.

Walking Tour

Walking around Sian, distances seem even longer than they are, probably because of the width of the streets and the absence of perspective afforded by high-rise buildings. For a short excursion, turn left outside the hotel gate, and left again at the first intersection. A walk along this street will convey a good flavor of urban living in this part of China—a remarkable contrast from Peking, Shanghai, or Kwangchow. After two long blocks, one reaches Tun Wu Road and the People's Park. Turning right, another long block ends at Chiehfang Road, Sian's major north-south boulevard. To the north is the railway station. Turning south, the walker passes through a shopping district. Upon reaching Tung Hsin Road, turn right again. On the right side, one block away, is the hotel.

HOTEL ACCOMMODATIONS

The People's Hotel, built in the late 1950s in leaden Soviet style, is Sian's only hotel for foreigners. It is located in the northeast section of town on Tung Hsin Street, a major east-west thoroughfare. Showing the effects of underuse, its atmosphere is rather forlorn and uninviting. Increased tourism can be expected to make the place more lively and, perhaps, the service more efficient.

The lobby has a service desk, bank, and post office combined, and a small retail shop for local handicrafts. The rooms are ample, with deep tubs in the bathrooms (as in all Chinese hotels there are only hand-held shower heads which must be used while seated in the tub, a skill quickly mastered).

SIAN CUISINE

The food in Sian is noticeably plainer than in other parts of China which, if nothing else, makes for an interesting contrast. Mutton (disdained by northerners) is a staple in this part of the country, as are river fish. Since Shensi is wheat country, noodles predominate as a source of starch, although a coarse-grained rice is also served at the hotel.

SHOPPING

Recommended purchases include weavings and cotton goods (note: these are rationed in China, and a guide is needed to arrange such purchases). Products from local handicrafts and enamelware factories are available, as are stone rubbings.

Loyang

Now chiefly an agricultural center, Loyang was the capital of China during the Han and Chou dynasties. It is located about 120 km. (75 mi.) east of Sian, at the confluence of the Wei and Yellow rivers. It has a population of 700,000.

The site of Loyang has been inhabited since Chinese history began, with neolithic remains dating from the Yang and Shang cultures. Parts of the wall built during the Han Dynasty still stand. During the Sui Dynasty (606 AD), the city became known as an artistic and cultural center.

Modern Loyang is famous for its tractor plant— the first to be built in China. In addition, there are machinery works, a ball-bearing factory, and glass works. In 1949, the city had only 100 industrial workers; presently there are 150,000, including 25,000 at the tractor plant. Chief agricultural products of the region include corn, wheat, cotton, and livestock.

The most famous tourist site in Loyang is the Lungmen Cave, a monument to Buddhist influence in China during the 6th century. The cave has a number of carvings, dominated by a 45-ft. statue of Buddha sitting in the lotus position. The torso and hands have been eroded by time and weather, but the chest and head are in fine condition and every imposing. A nearby cave has some 10,000 bodhisattvas carved into the wall.

Other highlights of the itinerary include the tractor plant, Wang Cheng Park (the site of two Han Dynasty tombs), White Horse Temple (one of the first Buddhist temples in China), and the Loyang Municipal Museum (featuring artifacts discovered since 1949).

Tachai

Tachai is a small village in the Taihang Mountains in Shansi Province. It is situated near the city of Yangchuan. Tachai is on the China traveler's itinerary not by virtue of any great historical sights or even contemporary edifices, but because it exemplifies China's revolutionary principles put into practice. Tachai was once a poverty-stricken rural area marked by rock-strewn hills, poor soil, and flood-prone valleys. The area has now become highly productive farmland, well-irrigated and terraced, and supportive of forestry and animal husbandry, as well as agriculture. As a result, the Tachai Production Brigade has become the standard-bearer for agricultural production in China. Its enormous success prompted Mao to press for a nationwide "Learn-from-Tachai" campaign. Recently, the leadership has called for the massive transformation of China's rural counties into "Tachai-type" units. In 1975 and 1976, "Learn-from-Tachai" conferences set forth plans to convert one-third of China's counties into "Tachai-type" units by 1980.

Measured by any criteria, the achievement of Tachai is significant. Tachai's original agricultural cooperative was set up in 1953 when 50 men and women set out literally to transform nature without recourse to mechanization or advanced technology. Collective production succeeded in doubling the output of the land over when it was divided into individual plots. In 1958, a people's commune was established with the Tachai community designated as one of its production brigades. Local peasants terraced the mountain slopes with picks and shovels and quarried rock with hammers and chisels in order to build embankments that would keep the mountain gullies from flooding over. They moved huge quantities of fertile soil from other localities to create viable farmlands within embankments.

The most arduous task was the construction of the commune's longest irrigation gully (1.5 km.), called Langsochang (Wolf's Pad). During the winter of 1955, the people built 38 stone embankments along the gully and created terraced fields suitable for farming. However, summer flooding washed away these efforts. The embankments were rebuilt, only to be destroyed again by torrential floods during the summer of 1957. Unwilling to admit defeat, the brigade decided to try again, this time constructing embankments in curved rows with deeper foundations and larger boulders. Inspired by the determination of the local brigade, many other commune members pitched in to complete the embankments along the gully and collect the tens of thousands of cubic meters of fertile soil needed to create 44 terraced fields. Thus the project was completed (three days ahead of schedule). It has withstood storms and floods since 1957 and now boasts the highest agricultural yield in the area.

Today, Tachai has a varied crop output, electricity, aerial cableways, processing equipment, irrigation machinery, and new housing. It has ample grain reserves and is able to produce a surplus for sale to the state.

Chengchow

kingdom of Cheng
Pinyin Spelling: Zhengzhou ("chung-joe")

Chengchow is the capital of Honan Province and a major city in north-central China. It is located a few miles south of the Yellow River and is about 640 km. (400 mi.) due south of Peking. Geographically, it sits at the western edge of the agriculturally important North China Plain.

A major railway center that links Kwangchow and Peking (on the north-south axis) and Sian and Shanghai (on the east-west axis), Chengchow continues in its traditional role as a major market and transportation center. Infrequently visited by tourists in the past, it is becoming an increasingly more common stop because of its central location and its example as a well-planned town with balanced development of agriculture and industry. All told, Chengchow provides a powerful visual symbol of the rebuilding that has taken place in new China.

The population of 900,000 enjoys a pleasant climate in spring and autumn, but midsummer temperatures soar above 90°F, with heavy rains occurring in July.

Chengchow in History

Chengchow has a long history, having been continuously settled for more than 3,000 years. It ranked as one of the most populous regions in China during the Shang Dynasty (ca. 1760-1100 BC), but for a period thereafter waned in importance because of the proximity of Loyang, which emerged as the dynastic capital.

The modern development of the city began in 1898 when foreign interests were granted concessions for the construction of major north-south and east-west rail lines. These were completed in 1910. In the 1920s, the railway was the focus of several labor disputes, including a notorious incident on February 7, 1923, when a strike against the local warlord was bloodily suppressed. Because of its importance as a major railway center, Chengchow was a primary objec-

149

tive of Japanese forces during their push through China in 1937. In an infamous incident now memorialized locally, the Kuomintang (Nationalist) army breached the dike of the Yellow River less than 20 miles northeast of the city in order to deny it to the Japanese. The action resulted in devastating floods that cost thousands of lives through drowning or subsequent starvation. The diverted river continued to threaten the city until 1947, when the break was repaired through US assistance. Chengchow was again severely damaged in fighting that took place during the Civil War in 1948-49. Labor troubles resurfaced in the 1970s, and local officials speak of the "sabotage carried out by the 'gang of four' and their henchmen."

Economy and Culture

Chengchow was initially rebuilt during 1949-50, but significant urban expansion did not take place until after 1954 when the city was designated as a site for concerted industrial development. Food-processing and cotton textile industries were given priority. By the 1960s, Chengchow had become an important industrial center as well as a transportation hub.

The textile sector includes five mills that produce both yarn and finished cloth. Associated facilities include a textile printing and dyeing plant and several textile machinery plants. Food and agricultural industries include a meat-processing and by-products plant, flour mills, and a plant that processes cottonseed into edible oil and other products. Chemical fertilizer, insecticides, and tractor repair plants (the region's flat terrain makes it ideal for agricultural mechanization) are also located in Chengchow. Major agricultural products are rice, wheat, and cottonseed.

Chengchow has 175 primary schools, 42 secondary schools, and 13 technical schools. Technical schools specialize in medicine, architecture, commerce, forestry, hydraulic engineering, and agriculture. The city maintains 8 theaters and 13 cinemas.

HIGHLIGHTS FOR TRAVELERS

Although Chengchow's tourist attractions do not rival those of Shanghai, Sian, or Peking, it is nevertheless a city of considerable interest. Most of the city is modern in appearance, reflecting its tremendous growth since 1950 (when its population was 100,000 and had only five factories employing 700 workers). In the new section of town, blocks of governmental, educational, and cultural buildings are intermingled with extensive residential areas. There are broad, tree-lined avenues and a variety of monumental civic structures.

There is also an old town core, with narrow, maze-like streets and traditional houses that serve as a reminder of other times. Some housing foundations and graves from the 3rd century BC have been discovered in this old section, and remnants of the ancient wall still stand.

☐ **Cenotaph.** In the heart of the shopping district of the old section stands a cenotaph built to commemorate the bloody general strike of railroad workers in February 1923.

☐ **Honan Provincial Museum.** Located in the newer section of town, the museum contains exhibitions from the neolithic period, early dynasties, and the modern period, including the railway strikes, war of resistance against the Japanese, the civil war, and post-1949 developments. Artifacts from early dynasties include tools from Yang and Shang cultures, lacquerware, wooden figurines, bronzes, and textiles from tomb sites dating from the Chou and Six Dynasties era, bronzes from the T'ang Dynasty, and samples of pottery from the Sung. All artifacts were discovered in Honan Province.

☐ **Textile Mills.** To demonstrate the comprehensive development of modern China, factories, communes, and educational institutions are included on the itinerary of most visitors. Chengchow's textile mills are among the most advanced in China. Leading members of factory management committees often remark with pride about how the "old" Chengchow has been transformed.

☐ **People's Park.** Just behind the Opera Theater, this park has pleasant walkways and a lake fed by the Chin-shui River, which is connected by a canal to the Yellow River to the north. The Park serves as a rough dividing line between the old and new towns, with the city's major department store just one black south and workers' residential areas situated immediately to the north.

HOTEL ACCOMMODATIONS

Most visitors will be put up at the Honan Hotel, a grand structure built in Soviet style, with a large fountain in front, a cavernous lobby, and a huge, red-carpeted marble staircase. The massive external scale telescopes into small but comfortable rooms. The hotel has the usual tourist amenities, including a retail shop (with relatively sparse selection), telegraph and post offices, and bank. The building is surrounded on three sides by wheat fields. During harvest times, many of the hotel employees leave to join in the agricultural work.

Since the hotel stands on the outskirts of town, it may give the visitor a feeling of isolation. The cenotaph, marking Chengchow's center, is a good 45-minute (two-mile) walk, as is the People's Park.

SHOPPING

The lapidary shop is a standard part of the itinerary. Jade from several provinces is sold here. Linens and textiles are also a good buy. Handicrafts feature egg-shell painting, feather painting, and stuffed animals. Since the store in the hotel is not well-stocked (as of 1976), a trip to the Chengchow Department Store and local specialty shops is recommended. There is no Friendship Store in Chengchow.

Wuhan

"Wuhan" is a contraction of three city names—"Wu" from Wuchang and "han" from Hankow and Hanyang

Pinyin Spelling: Wuhan ("woo-hahn")

Wuhan, the capital of Hupei Province, is the collective name given to the three closely-linked municipalities—Wuchang, Hankow, and Hanyang. The three cities were physicially connected in 1957 upon completion of the Changchiang Bridge, the first and only span to cross the Yangtse between Chungking to the west and Nanking to the east (prior to 1957, all of China's north-south railway traffic had to be ferried across the river). Located in central China, in the middle of the Yangtse Plain, Wuhan is roughly 1,000 miles from each of China's four large cities: Peking and Kwangchow (on a north-south axis) and Shanghai and Chungking (on an east-west axis).

Wuhan is situated at the confluence of the Han and Yangtse rivers. Its three urban sections have a combined population of 1,900,000 people, with an additional 600,000 residing in the suburbs. It is the foremost city in a region noted for its population density and heavy industry. Wuhan is also a major transportation center. As an inland port, it can handle 8,000-ton vessels coming up river from Shanghai, some 1,000 miles away. It is also a key rail center.

Wuhan's three urban components have similar geographical features in that they are all situated on low, flat land and interspersed with numerous ponds, canals, and other waterways. Formerly vulnerable to flooding, much of this threat has been diminished by a newly reinforced series of dikes.

Wuhan's strategic location has also made it the third most important military center in China, a role that has considerable historical precedence. Battles fought here at the turn of the century accompanied the fall of the Ch'ing Dynasty. In 1949, Communist forces in this sector won key victories over the last pockets of Kuomintang resistance, paving the way to final victory.

153

Wuhan in History

Hankow. Hankow occupies the northwest section of Wuhan, bordered by the Yangtse on the east and the Han River to the south. Hankow began as a fishing village (with origins as early as the 3rd century BC) and it remained so until the mid-19th century. Under terms of the Treaty of Nanking (1861), it was designated a treaty port and its status gradually began to change as foreign firms began to open branches. However, it was not until the building of the railway in the first decade of the 20th century that Hankow began truly to expand. In the course of its rapid industrial buildup, Hankow became the scene of the bloody "February 7th" strike of 1923, the first large-scale industrial strike in modern China history. Today, Hankow is the most modern section of Wuhan and the site of an important military installation.

Hanyang. Located south of the Han River and west of the Yangtse, Hanyang is the smallest of Wuhan's three municipalities. It was founded as a municipality about 600 AD. The city gained prominence in the late 19th century as a focal point for political reform. Hanyang's political leaders were part of a movement that sought to revitalize China through "self-strengthening"—it was felt that by learning from the West rather than ignoring it, China could become strong enough to oust the foreign powers. Within the industrial sector, this policy led directly to the construction in Hanyang of China's first modern iron and steel complex in 1891. By the early 1900s, an arsenal and several other factories had been added along Hanyang's river front. The city's industrialization program collapsed during the depression of the 1930s. During the Sino-Japanese War (1937-45), much of the industry that remained was destroyed. Since 1949, however, the area has entered a new era as a center for light industry.

Wuchang. Wuchang, located on the eastern side of the Yangtse, is the oldest of the three municipalities and has long functioned as an administrative center for the region. In the 14th century (during the Yuan Dynasty), Wuchang served as the capital of a large administrative region (encompassing what are now four central provinces). Today, it serves as the administrative seat for Hupei Province.

On October 10, 1911, the first victorious battle of the 1911 Revolution took place in Wuchang (Sun Yat-sen himself was absent—he was in Hawaii raising funds for the revolution). The site of the battle is commemorated by a bronze statue of Sun (on Shouyi Road). The

Central Institute of the Peasant Movement, an important political training ground during the early years of the Chinese Communist movement, was set up in Wuchang. It was headed by Mao himself in 1927.

Economy and Culture

The name Wuhan is metaphorically synonymous with iron and steel as it is the site of some of China's most important foundries (surpassed only by the Anshan complex). With the assistance of West German and Japanese engineers, the Wuhan Iron and Steel Complex is being expanded to include a 3,000,000-metric-ton steel rolling mill. The area also produces a substantial array of chemicals, fertilizers, construction materials, and railway ties, as well as cotton fabrics and a number of light industrial products. An open-pit iron mine about 65 km. (40 mi.) southeast of Wuhan (Taiyeh Iron Ore Mines) provides almost all of Wuhan's iron ore (and limestone).

Although Wuhan is not primarily an agricultural region, rice and cotton output have increased greatly as the area strives to attain self-sufficiency. The growing season lasts 300 days and permits two yearly crops of both wheat and tea. Freshwater fisheries also contribute to the local economy.

Wuhan is above all else a working city and most aspects of its cultural life relate to this characteristic. Given its long history of intensive settlement and commercial activity, Wuhan retains visible links to the major cultural and political currents of China from at least the times of the T'ang emperors. In a country that today stresses political evolution and economic development above all other goals, Wuhan's pace and lifestyle are telling indicators of the direction China now seeks for its industrial centers.

HIGHLIGHTS FOR TRAVELERS

Hankow

The most modern of the Wuhan municipalities, Hankow serves as a model for Chinese urban planning. Its broad tree-lined boulevards are flanked by modern apartment houses, offices, and landscaped parks.

The city's legacy from the days of Western occupation is still visible along the Yenchiang Tatao, a street that runs parallel to the Yangtse in the northeast section. As with the Bund in Shanghai, government offices now occupy what were once banks, department stores, and palatial homes. Tourist sites include the Handicrafts Display Center, Sun Yat-sen (Chung Shan) Park (formerly a race track), the Institute of Medicine, and the Wuhan Zoo.

Hanyang

Hanyang, a densely-populated district made up of a jumble of one-story, slate-roofed houses, is typical of old Chinese cities. The low-lying area just south of the Han River is now Hanyang's industrial district, connected to Hankow by the Changchiang Bridge. As Hanyang was formerly a popular residential retreat for the area's gentry, it includes numerous reminders of those eras.

☐ **Lotus Lake (Lienhua Lu).** This small, picturesque lake, now cast in the shadows of the Changchiang Bridge, was formerly the site of a European settlement.

☐ **Tortoise Hill (Kuei Shan).** So named because of its resemblance to a tortoise, it is the only hill of any size in Wuhan. The area includes a well-maintained park and many points of interest, including pavilions, caverns, and a former monastery. One can now scale the "mountain" by means of stone steps.

☐ **Workers' Cultural Palace.** The Palace is the focal point of a park that also contains the Terrace of the Ancient Lute, overlooking gardens and the river.

Wuchang

The old part of Wuchang clings to a low ridge (She Shan—Serpent Hill), along which runs the railway spur that bisects the municipality. The old flavor of the city is well-preserved in its northern section, with modern offices and industrial areas relegated to the south.

☐ **Yangtse River Bridge (Changchiang Bridge).** This bridge, along with its counterpart in Nanking, was built under "impossible" geological conditions, and is regarded as a symbol of China's modern industrial progress and self-reliance. The first modern bridge to span the Yangtse, it was completed on September 25, 1957 (two years ahead of schedule). Both levels of the structure are flanked by broad sidewalks for pedestrians and bicycles. The lower deck supports the railway; the upper, six lanes of vehicular traffic. The bridge is 1,156 m. (3,792 ft.) long, and reaches 80 m. (263 ft.) above the water. It has 8 piers and 9 spans.

☐ **Hsiang Pagoda.** The Hsiang Pagoda, also known as Yellow Crane Tower (Huang He Lou), was erected in the beginning of the 3rd century AD, and is the main attraction in the park that surrounds Serpent Hill (She Shan). Through the verse of the T'ang Dynasty poet Tsui Han, the Pagoda attained repute for the panoramic view it affords (now an ideal spot to survey the bridge). Since its construction, it has been restored three times, most recently by the present government which retained its Ming and Ch'ing dynasty elements.

☐ **Site of the Central Institute of the Peasant Movement.** Prior to the founding of the PRC, the Communist Party built an institute to train cadres and organize peasants. Its headmaster in 1927 was Mao Tse-tung. This site now houses Middle School No. 22. However, Mao's former residence and some classrooms have been preserved and are open to the public.

☐ **East Lake (Tung Hu).** Larger than Lake Tai and several times the size of Hangchow's West Lake, this picturesque lake is surrounded by a park covering 94 sq. km. (36.3 sq. mi.). Among the park's numerous tourist sites are the Ting Tao Temple—the Taoist master Lao Tzu's place of meditation; Lung Tsuen (Dragon Spring); the Hsing Ying Court— a pavilion in a wooded area commemorating the ancient poet Chu Yuan; and the Chiu Nu Tuen (Tomb of the Nine Heroines).

The Hupei Provincial Museum, noted for displays of recent archeological excavations, traces the province's history from its origins to the Opium War

HOTEL ACCOMMODATIONS

The Wuhan Hotel is a structure in the old style, located in the heart of Hankow.

WUHAN CUISINE

The Yangtse River serves not only as a geographical boundary but also as a gastronomic border. The staple north of the river is noodles whereas to the south rice predominates along with more elaborately flavored dishes. The Wuhan area is noted for its fresh fish and wild ducks from East Lake.

Shih Chia Chuang

Sheltered by the Taihang Mountains to the west and bordered by the fertile Hopei plain which fans out on its three other sides, Shih Chia Chuang is a railway junction on the Peking-Kwangchow line, about

150 mi. south of Peking. It has a population of 450,000. The city owes its existence almost entirely to the railway; before its contruction in 1905, there was only a village of 500-600 people. The other major industry in the town is cotton milling.

Shih Chia Chuang is of special interest to Canadian visitors because its hospital is dedicated to the memory of Dr. Norman Bethune, a Canadian surgeon who came to China in the 1930s to assist the Communist cause. He is still revered in China as a model of selfless sacrifice. His tomb lies in the cemetery just west of the town. Coincidentally, the cemetery is also the site of one of the few historical objects of interest in Shih Chia Chuang, two bronze lions dating from 1185.

The Shih Chia Chuang Guest House is located in the southwest corner of the city. A few blocks north is the Tung Fang Hung ("East is Red") Exhibition Hall, featuring displays of local products.

CENTRAL CHINA

Yenan

south of the Yen River
Pinyin Spelling: Yan'an ("Yeh-nan")

Yenan, a market town of 30,000 people, is located some 270 km. (168 mi.) north of Sian in Shensi Province. Having served as the headquarters of the Communist Party from 1936-47, it is symbolically and historically one of the most revered sites in the People's Republic.

The Yen River cuts a deep path between the dry loess hills, repositories of the innumerable cave dwellings characteristic of the area. The hills have been extensively terraced to provide an agricultural base for the local economy.

Other than sites connected with the revolution, the city has few standard tourist attractions. There are several factories, a university, and an assortment of historical sites (Buddhist caves, a Taoist hermitage, and a Sung Dynasty pagoda—the town's symbol). The main points of interest are the Museum of the Revolution and the caves

Yenan

where Mao Tse-tung and other Chinese leaders directed the revolution during its "Yenan Period."

Yenan in History

In 1936, the Communist Eighth Route Army staggered into this protected area at the end of one of the great epics in military history—the 8,000-mile Long March, a two-and-a-half-year trek through central and western China that survived the incessant ravages of climate, terrain, and numerous encounters with the Nationalist forces of Chiang Kai-shek. It was during the Long March that Mao Tse-tung consolidated his control of the Party, and it was in Yenan that Mao, Chou En-lai, Chu Teh, and others reassessed the failures of the formerly urban-based revolution and forged the political and military strategies that led to victory in the civil war and the establishment of the People's Republic of China.

The ordeals of the Long March had compelled its leaders to place survival ahead of orthodox doctrine. Once in Yenan, ideology was again tempered by circumstances. The concerns of class struggle paled before the need to mount a national war of resistance against Japan. Appealing to the latent nationalism of the rural population, the Party began to rebuild itself on a peasant base. The Red Army gained considerable support for its guerrilla campaigns. Its ranks swelled by peasant volunteers, the Army became a strong, cohesive force, both politically and militarily.

The Yenan Legacy. The specific policies developed at Yenan succeeded in winning broad, enthusiastic support from the peasantry. Indeed, their contribution to the eventual success of the revolution prompted the continued application of many of these policies (e.g., through land reform and mass mobilizations) throughout Mao's 28 years at the helm of the People's Republic. (Indeed, the Great Proletarian Cultural Revolution of 1966-68 may be seen in part as an attempt to re-infuse the Yenan spirit into the workings of government.) The main theoretical legacies from Yenan may be characterized as:

1. Heavy reliance on the creativity of the "masses," particularly the peasantry, in their ability to overcome the ravages of nature, poverty, and political exploitation;

2. Rejection of administrative control through a closed, unresponsive, and elitist bureaucracy;

3. Periodic rotation of intellectuals and other elites to the countryside for periods of manual labor so as to break down barriers between them and the masses (i.e., workers and peasants);

4. Reliance on cooperative movements to reorganize local economies (forerunners of the commune system);

5. Development of a mass culture and education movement whose primary aim was the integration of literature, art, and formal schooling with politics.

Since 1977, the leadership's emphasis on modernization has led, in many instances, to a more circumspect approach to these policies, although their themes continue to be interwoven in political pronouncements. Yenan had been a frequent stop on the itinerary of foreign groups in the 1960s and early 1970s (particularly politically-oriented delegations), but has since been less often visited.

[Readers are referred to Mark Selden's *The Yenan Way in Revolutionary China* (Harvard University Press, 1971) and to Fairbank, Reischauer, and Craig's *East Asia: The Modern Transformation* (Houghton Mifflin Company, 1956) for a more detailed account of the Yenan legacy.]

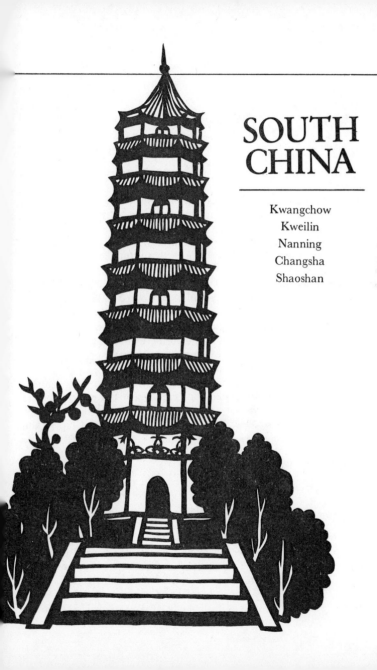

SOUTH CHINA

Kwangchow
Kweilin
Nanning
Changsha
Shaoshan

Kwangchow

broad region

Pinyin Spelling: Guangzhou ("guahng-joe")

Kwangchow, the capital of Kwangtung Province, is the most important industrial city in southern China and one of the country's chief trade outlets. While some visitors have found the city ungraceful and cluttered, its lush parks, tree-lined streets, leisurely pace, and distinctive cuisine have lent it a character that is unique among China's large cities.

The municipality of Kwangchow covers an area of some 4,330 sq. km. (1,678 sq.mi.) and has a population of over 3 million—including 2 million in the city itself and 1 million in the surrounding six counties. Known for many years as Canton by Westerners and Chinese alike, Kwangchow is located at the northern edge of the Pearl River Delta, some 182 km. (75 mi.) northeast of Hong Kong by rail and 2,234 km. (1,443 mi.) directly south of Peking.

As China's focal point for foreign trade, the city hosts the semiannual Chinese Export Commodities Fair which attracts more than 25,000 businessmen. It is also the country's principal tourist gateway. During the Chinese New Year, some 200,000 overseas Chinese and Hong Kong residents visit relatives and friends in the area.

Kwangchow in History

According to legend, Kwangchow was founded by five celestial beings riding goats who arrived bearing grain for the people. The legend stuck, to the extent that until the late 1950s the Tung Fang Hotel was known (in a complimentary way) as the Goat Hotel. "Goat Brand" bicycles are manufactured here, and a modern statue of the five goats still proudly surmounts a hill in Yue Hsi Park.

As early as the 9th century BC, Kwangchow was known as Chu Ting. It received its present name in the 3rd century BC. In 714 AD, the T'ang Dynasty set up a bureau in the city to handle overseas trade, thus designating it as the first officially-sanctioned foreign trade port in China. As such, Kwangchow was also the first Chinese city to experience an unsettling influx of Christian, Muslim, and other foreign influences. Although the city was enriched both by periodic migrations from northern China and by influences from abroad, the local culture remained fiercely independent, with its own dialect, literature, music, customs, and sense of identity.

Kwangchow fell most directly under Western influences in the 19th century. Western commercial settlements, with their spacious buildings and large compounds, sharply set off the poor housing and cluttered canals of the main city. Modernization of the city began in the 1920s when canals were filled and rows of buildings demolished to make way for wider boulevards. A police system was set up and public health facilities were expanded. A new wave of construction began under the Communist government, which added parks, industrial sites, and modern harbor facilities.

Role in the Chinese Revolution. In 1757, Kwangchow became the country's only government-sanctioned foreign trade port. Thus, Kwangchow was destined to become a major point of confrontation between Western expansionism of the 19th century and the struggle for national identity within China. During the period 1839-1927, the Cantonese were at the forefront of several of China's reform movements and revolutionary activities. The city had developed rapidly as China's export center for silks, tea, spices, and other items prized on European markets. To finance these purchases, the British sold opium (produced under their rule in India) to the Chinese. China tried to halt this by imperial decree in 1839. When that device failed, officials ordered the opium confiscated and publicly burned. The British, anxious for a pretext, took this act as just grounds for initiating military action. Britain's victory in the resulting Opium War (1839-42) led to the Treaty of Nanking, which compelled China to open four additional treaty ports along its coast. Coupled with the threat from the West, China was also experiencing a period of social and economic dislocation associated with dynastic decline. The Taiping Rebellion, a movement of the 1860s, was led by a Cantonese (Hung Hsiu-ch'uan). Cantonese were also at the forefront of the national government reform movement of the 1890s.

Sun Yat-sen, a native son of Kwangchow (and still nominally revered in China today), was the father of the revolution of 1911 that succeeded in overthrowing the imperial system. As the seat of China's Republican government in the early 1920s and the site of Sun's founding of the Kuomintang (Nationalist) Party in 1923, Kwangchow be-

KWANGCHOW (CANTON)

15 Moslem Restaurant	**23** Peasant Movement Institute
16 Pei Yuan Restaurant	**24** Sun Yat-sen Memorial Hall
17 Snake	**25** Kwangchow Gymnasium
18 Chen Hai Tower	**26** Yue Hsi Stadium
19 Statue of Five Goats	**27** Antique Shops
20 Hai Chu Square	**28** Friendship Store
21 Huai Sheng Mosque	**29** Nan Fang Department Store
22 Kwangchow Uprising Memorial	

came a focal point of political resurgence, with the Communists gaining early strength there. In the spring of 1927, the Kuomintang launched an extermination campaign against the Communists, who responded by fomenting the "Canton Uprising." Although the insurgents succeeded in occupying government offices and leading a general strike, the revolt was put down in three days. Communist activity in the region was not again a factor until the advent of the Sino-Japanese War, when guerrilla forces worked to undermine the invasion. Of Kwangchow's role in the revolution, contemporary PRC accounts relate that the "people of Kwangchow launched one after another heroic struggles against the invasion and oppression by imperialism, feudalism, and comprador capitalism."

Economy and Culture

The rich alluvial area of the Pearl River Delta provides the Kwangchow region with a highly productive agricultural base. Today, some 92,000 hectares (227,000 acres) are under cultivation. In addition to three yearly rice crops, the area produces wheat, fruit, vegetables, sugarcane, and oil-yielding plants. Within Kwangchow itself there are 33 communes and 16 state farms.

Kwangchow's major industrial products are newsprint, refined sugar, ships, cement, steel, chemicals, automobiles, machinery, textiles, rubber goods, and canned foods. The industrial sector comprises about 2,000 enterprises employing a total of 500,000 workers. The average rate of growth since 1966 has been estimated at 9.5% per year, with the total value of industrial output rising by 213% from 1966 to 1975. Priority has been given to steel (up 198%); automobiles (up 477% since 1971), chemical fibers (up 500%), and shipbuilding. The city is also important for its light industrial products, although this sector has grown more slowly. Among the key products are clothing (about one-third of which is exported), bamboo and rattan products, pottery, ivory, jade, and jewelry.

There are 98 hospitals (2 used by foreigners) with 13,700 beds, supplemented by 1,120 medical and health-care units. Long a center of education, Kwangchow has 11 colleges and research institutes, the most famous of which is Chungshan ("Sun Yat-sen University"). There are 1,169 primary and middle schools attended by 770,000 students. In addition, the city has a nationally-renowned museum, a library, and a botanical garden.

HIGHLIGHTS FOR TRAVELERS

☐ **Yue Hsi Park.** Located just east of the Tung Fang Hotel, this 247-acre park with its hills and artificial lakes is an ideal place to begin a tour of Kwangchow. The most famous landmark within the park is the Chen Hai Tower, rising five stories (28 meters) and presenting a commanding view of the city. Built in 1380 (during the Ming Dynasty) and rebuilt in 1686 as a lookout post (its name means "overlooking the seas"), the tower underwent extensive renovation in the 1950s and now serves as the Kwangchow Municipal Museum.

Start the visit by climbing to the top story. Tea is served on a veranda that looks out over the city. The walk down winds through thousands of years of Chinese pottery, starting with the neolithic period and ending, on the second floor, with the modern products of Kwangtung factories. During the Export Commodities Fair, and sometimes during the summer months, students from the Kwangchow Foreign Languages Institute often act as informal guides, approaching the visitor with a request to practice their English, Spanish, French, or German. The small garden in front of the museum has a pair of 19th-century Krupp canons.

Also located in Yue Hsi Park are some of Kwangchow's excellent athletic facilities, including a stadium (seating 40,000 and often used for political rallies), two Olympic pools (open to foreigners in the early morning), and badminton courts. There are many walkways through the park, a place for renting boats, pavilions for viewing the lake, and a garden restaurant. In late fall, a Crysanthemum Festival is staged here, with some plants producing over 1,500 individual blossoms.

☐ **Liu Hua Park.** Liu Hua Park flanks the Tung Fang Hotel on the west side, and its artificial lake, palm-lined walkways, bowed bridges, and resting pavilions make it popular for a casual stroll.

☐ **Memorial Garden to the Martyrs of the Canton Uprising (Hung Hua Kuang).** This Memorial Park commemorates the Communist-led uprising of workers and farmers of December 11, 1927. Kuomintang reprisals resulted in 5,000 casualties. The garden was laid out in 1954 and officially opened in 1957, on the 30th anniversary of the Uprising. It covers 64 acres, and is entered through a rather impressive gate.

☐ **Mausoleum of the 72 Martyrs at Huang Hua Kang.** The revolution that overthrew the Ch'ing Dynasty was actually a series of uprisings, ten of which failed. This Mausoleum commemorates one abortive attempt, the uprising of March 29, which resulted in the loss of 72 lives. The site was originally constructed in 1918 by funds donated by overseas Chinese.

☐ **National Peasant Movement Institute.** Founded in July 1924 on the site of a former Confucian temple, this school was used by the fledgling Communist Party to train cadres for the revolution. Many leaders of the Communist movement, such as Chou En-lai and Kuo Mo-jo, taught there. Its most famous headmaster was Mao Tse-tung. Visitors are shown a replica of his room and various memorabilia. The Institute trained 327 students in 1926, but was shut down as part of the reprisals in connection with the Canton Uprising.

☐ **Huai Sheng Mosque.** Dating from 627 AD, this is regarded as the oldest mosque in China, and is still used for religious activities. It was reportedly built by the first person to bring the Koran to China, said to be an uncle of Mohammed. Built in Islamic style, the mosque has an 80-foot minaret and two levels.

☐ **Liu Yung Temple.** Constructed in 479 AD, it is also known as the Temple of the Six Banyan Trees. Partially destroyed by fire in 1098, the present name owes its origins to a famous poet of the time, Su Tung-po, who was struck by the presence of six banyan trees on the grounds. The trees are gone, but there is still an octagonal-based pagoda (Hua Tower) with one of those feats for which Chinese architects were famous: 9 stories on the outside and 17 on the inside. The tower is 57 m. (188 ft.) high.

☐ **Cultural Park.** Just a block from the Pearl River, the Kwangchow Cultural Park is a focal-point for mass culture. Rebuilt in 1952, its 20 acres include an excellent aquarium (the Pearl River Delta display, featuring various local species, is remarkable for its variety), seven exhibition halls, flower gardens, theater, opera house, concert hall, and stadium. There is also a roller-skating rink, a tea house, and facilities for table tennis. Admission to the park is 10 fen, but cultural events and concerts require separate tickets available only from the host organization.

☐ **Kwangchow Zoo.** The Kwangchow Zoo is one of China's four largest, and rivals that of Peking in its varieties of over 200 species. Most popular, predictably, are the panda bears, but also worth seeing are the displays of monkeys, giraffes, hippopotamus, camels, tigers, and an aviary. The zoo has a restaurant, snack bar, and small retail shop. It is open 7:30 AM to 3:30 PM daily. Admission is 10 fen.

□ **Sha Mien.** Although it is not the kind of historical site tour guides are likely to recommend, a walk around Sha Mien will evoke the spirit of the prerevolutionary days when this was the area of the British and French concessions. Built on an island in the river and accessible only by a narrow bridge, its large buildings—once housing banks, churches, and administration buildings—now present a rather forlorn appearance. They are presently used to house several municipal bureaus, a Polish shipping office, the Vietnamese Consulate, a seaman's club, and military barracks.

There are two restaurants on the island (Sheng Li and Economical), and the tennis courts can be used by Westerners with the persistence to sign up (regulations are posted). The promenade along the river bank is shaded by large banyan trees and makes a pleasant walk, especially to escape the summer heat.

Kwangchow Suburbs

□ **Foshan City.** An old city located ten miles southwest of Kwangchow, it is usually visited on a one-day trip. Formerly a religious center (the name means Buddha Hill), it is also famous for its pottery, which is the main industry of Foshan today. Visitors are taken for a tour of the factory, followed by a visit to a shop featuring examples of local pottery (look for the tiny natural clay sampans, or the three-inch glazed pandas). Lunch is usually served in a large old hotel. The afternoon is taken up by a visit to the site of a former Taoist Temple, now somewhat gaudily restored but housing a number of statues and artifacts from the Ming Dynasty.

□ **Seven Star Crags.** The local tour guides will boast that this area combines the lakes of Hangchow with the mountains of Kweilin. Although this might raise expectations a bit high, the several-square-mile area is nevertheless worth the three-hour bus ride (62 miles, including a ferry crossing), especially if there is time to spend the night. The local tea is unusual and the entire area is splendid for photography.

□ **Hot Springs (Tsung Hua).** Also several hours from the city, the Kwangtung Hot Springs—with its curative waters (112° F)—are a tonic for those spending time in Kwangchow during the hectic trade fairs. A visit usually entails a weekend excursion.

Seven Star Crags

☐ **White Cloud Mountain (Pai Yun Shan).** This 1,400-foot hill is the highest point in the region. It affords a panoramic view of Kwangchow, the Pearl River, and the entire delta region. Pavilions and teahouses, situated at the summit, encourage a lingering view. Further down the hill are a number of luxurious hotels—the most extravagant to be seen in China. Large villas are appointed with sitting rooms, sunken baths, private gardens, streams, ponds, and bamboo groves. These hotels are used both by high-ranking foreigners and by government officials. Since the hill also bristles with defense installations, walkers need to follow well-marked paths. A hike from the Tung Fang Hotel to the top of the mountain will take about six hours.

WALKING TOURS

Kwangchow offers splendid opportunities for the walker, whether for shopping, strolling through parks, or observing the everyday life of the city and its people.

A good place to begin a walk is Yue Hsi Park. To get to there, turn right out of the main gate of the Tung Fang Hotel, and walk one block to the intersection of Chieh Fang Road (easily identified by the traffic circle). Turn left, and the park entrance is just a half block down on the east side of the street, easily identified by its large gate.

Once in the gate, a left turn will lead to the lake, pavilions, flower displays, and, just up the hill, a building for flower exhibitions and, still farther up, tea houses and athletic facilities.

Turning right at the entrance will lead the visitor to the swimming pools and up the hill to Chen Hai Tower (gravestones are now used as steps on the smaller paths).

A side entrance to the park, which leads more directly to the Chen Hai Tower, can be found by turning right at the traffic circle (i.e., south instead of north to the main entrance). A long block later (past what has been nicknamed the "bicycle restaurant"—because of its popularity with commuters) is another traffic circle, where one turns sharply left up the hill. A hundred yards past the entrance, a set of steps leads up a hill on the left; this leads directly to the statue of the five goats. Retrace these steps back down the hill and turn left again up the main road into the park. At the top of the hill, the Chen Hai Tower is on the left, the Kwangchow Stadium immediately in front. To the right, a path leads to a cenotaph affording another good view of the city.

Liu Hua Park offers less variation, but is ideal for a pleasant stroll. Turn left out of the main gate of the Tung Fang Hotel and cross the first intersection. The entrance is another 300 yards to the left. Its circular paths make it impossible to get lost.

Also within a half-hour to 45-minute walk from the Tung Fang Hotel (round trip) are the Kwangchow Railway Station, the Gymnasium, and the botanical (orchid) garden.

HOTEL ACCOMMODATIONS

Kwangchow has 55 hotels with some 12,000 guest rooms. Five are especially set aside for foreigners. For the overseas Chinese, it is the Hua Chiao, located on Haichu Square, just by the Pearl River. Japanese are generally accommodated at the Kwangchow Hotel, also on Haichu Square, while Americans and Europeans usually stay at the Tung Fang or Bai Yun hotels.

☐ **Tung Fang Hotel.** Built in 1954, the Tung Fang was the first introduction to China for many businessmen and thus carries a certain nostalgia. The old wing, presently under renovation for air-conditioning and general sprucing up, has 400 rooms, with an architecture reminiscent of Eastern Europe. Some rooms have balconies, and all have a desk, two easy chairs, dresser with mirror, nightstand, electric fan, mosquito netting, and a telephone. A new 11-story wing, completed in 1974, has 700 rooms. Although its has a "cleaner" look, some guests find it a bit antiseptic, preferring the red carpets and spaciousness of the old wing to the cement terrazzo floors and plain wood trim of the new.

The Tung Fang has some of the best service facilities in China, including three restaurants (the dining room of the 8th floor of the old wing is best, but is often reserved for special delegations), four retail shops, a bank, a post office, and telegraph and telex facilities. A "snack room"—affectionately known among China traders as the "Top of the Fang"—serves Chinese beer, wine, and spirits.

Service counters are located on each floor, and the helpful staff will take care of laundry, dry-cleaning, and long-distance telephone bookings. They will even do small sewing jobs or other miscellaneous repair work. Beer, soft drinks, mineral water, ice, and cigarettes are available.

At the main service desk, located on the ground floor of each wing, one can book restaurants, have business cards printed, and order film developed. Recreation facilities at the hotel include badminton, ping-pong, and billiards.

The Tung Fang is located on Ren Min Road, North, directly opposite the Trade Fair complex (telephone: 69900). Its rates per night are Y22-26 (US$12.50-15.10) for a single or double room, Y40 (US$23.25) for a two-room suite, and Y150 (US$87.09) for a deluxe apartment.

☐ **Bai Yun Hotel.** Opened in January 1977, the Bai Yun (White Cloud) Hotel is Kwangchow's newest, and was built both to ease the

Tung Fang Hotel

housing pressure on the Tung Fang and to accommodate the new wave of tourists expected in the city. Although many prefer the Tung Fang for its proximity to the Trade Fair complex, the 33-story, 776-room Bai Yun is handsome, with comfortable rooms and a restaurant that overlooks a pleasant inner courtyard. The service staff is good, and the hotel has complete service facilities, including a beauty shop and bank.

Its relatively remote location (in the northwest section of town, halfway between Yue Hsi park and the Kwangchow Zoo) affords a view of neighboring farmland and foothills, but it also requires a Y2 taxi ride to the Fair (buses are provided free of charge). A Friendship Store is planned across the street.

The Bai Yun is located on Huan Shi Road, East, about 3 mi. from the Trade Fair complex (telephone: 67700). Its rates per night are Y22-26 (US$12.50-15.10) for a single or double room and Y40 (US$23.25) for a suite.

KWANGCHOW (CANTONESE) CUISINE

If there is one thing in Kwangchow that threatens the pre-occupation with business, it is eating. Local statisticians avow that there are some 22,000 seats available for eating in the city, and it seems there are at least that many dishes and variations in how they are prepared.

Chinese chefs from Kwangtung Province have fanned out across the world over the years and have had to put up with ersatz varieties of local vegetables, meats, and spices. Not surprisingly, the dishes that have resulted bear little resemblance to the Kwangchow originals. In addition, Cantonese food has lately gained an undeserved "second rate" reputation since Hunan, Szechuan, and Peking cuisines have become part of the international gourmet's vocabulary. But even people from other parts of China will admit that Cantonese cooking, with its appeal to the eye and the vast subtleties of its flavors, is one of the gastronomic wonders of the world.

Like elsewhere in China, the dishes in Kwangchow vary noticeably with the seasons, with casseroles and soups prevalent in the chilly, damp winters, and light soups and less oily dishes favored during the hot summer months.

Compared to the local restaurants, food at the hotels is adequate at best, and there is no better way to spend an evening in Kwangchow than to muster a group and head off to a new find or an old favorite.

The procedure is simple: giving as much notice as possible, go to the main service desk of the hotel and fill out a "restaurant booking form." The hotel will make the reservation, advise of the suggested cost per person, and convey any special requests. Reservations at the restaurant will be listed on a blackboard according to hotel room number. Guests are escorted to the private dining room where tea is served and moist washcloths passed around. Additional food requests are discussed, beverages decided upon (beer and wine are *de riguer*—seasoned visitors stay away from the fiery spirits called *Mao tai*), and the dinner proceeds apace. It should be noted that restaurants close about 9 PM, and lingering diners are frowned upon.

Local guides list some 34 restaurants that have special sections set aside for foreign visitors.

□ **Pan Hsi.** The Pan Hsi is one of Kwangchow's loveliest restaurants, as well as its largest. A staff of 400 can accommodate up to 1,000 people. Dining rooms overlook the lake and gardens that surround the restaurant. The specialty here is dumplings, but that simple term does not do justice to their variety of sizes, tastes, and fillings, all elegantly presented in the shape of little animals and birds. Also try the winter-melon soup (in season), or the squash soup with tiny shrimp.

The Pan Hsi is located at Liwan Park (telephone: 20350).

□ **Pei Yuan.** This is another restaurant whose internal setting matches the food. Unpretentious from the outside, its courtyard surprises the visitor with its small brook, bamboo trees, leaded glass windows, and private dining rooms. Chicken, vegetables, and soups are memorable here, and the Pei Yuan is less expensive than the Pan Hsi or Ta Tung.

The Pei Yuan is located on Tengfeng Road, North (telephone: 32471).

□ **Ta Tung.** The Ta Tung has become a favorite among foreign traders who attend the Fair. Set in a bustling part of the city, the top floors are reserved for foreigners and overlook the Pearl River, whose sounds, lights, and water traffic provide a unique setting. Specialties of the house include roast pig (the skin is the delicacy; roasted to crisp perfection, it is dipped in bean sauce, salt, and sugar and combined with a scallion in a piece of steamed dough).

The Ta Tung is one of the more expensive eating places in Kwangchow, charging Y15 and up per person. It is located at Hsihao Kou (telephone: 88697).

Some other restaurants worth noting: The Kwangchow Restaurant (Wen Chang Street; telephone: 87136) stays open a bit later than most (until 9:30 or so), and serves a good variety of local dishes. For those who simply must have Western food, try the Economical Restaurant (Sha Mien; telephone: 88784), where the portions are large. Western as well as Chinese dishes are served at the Tai P'ing (Peking Road North; telephone: 32599), although the clientele is mostly Chinese. For the exotic, try the Snake Restaurant (Changlan Road; telephone: 24679), where the snakes are skinned in full view of the diners (to demonstrate freshness). The Yeh Wei Shang Restaurant (Peking Road; telephone: 30977) is euphemistically called the "Wild Flavor Fragrance Restaurant" but can be more appropriately translated as the "Wild Game Restaurant," since it serves every kind of game imaginable, and then some. Turtle is a Cantonese specialty, and may be found at the San Chu Restaurant (Nan Hua Road; telephone: 50844). Noodles—plain, sweet, spicy, crispy, and so on— are served at the Sha Ho (Sha Ho Road; telephone: 70965), located in a northeast suburb of Kwangchow. There are also Moslem (vegetarian), Hakka, Mongolian, and Kechia restaurants.

Other dishes not mentioned above but worth trying include stuffed crab claws (in season), deep-fried fish balls, chicken—with ginger, or steamed in tea leaves, and roast goose served with plum sauce.

SHOPPING

The Friendship Store is a standard stop on the tourist itinerary. Since Kwangchow is also a major area for antiques, browsing in local stores is well recommended.

☐ **Friendship Store.** Located at 30 Yuang Kiang Road, just across from the Cultural Park and near Sha Mien, the Friendship Store is not likely to overwhelm the visitor. Its one large room offers only a limited sampling of the linens, textiles, ivory, jewelry, and arts and crafts that ordinarily make shopping in Kwangchow attractive. Suitcases are a useful purchase for those with bags already bulging from souvenirs. Ivory and linen are the only items not to be found elsewhere in the city. The store is open from 9 AM to 9 PM, and has a banking office to facilitate currency exchange.

☐ **Kwangchow Antique Shop and Kwangchow Antique Warehouse.** Although both places are recommended for antique hunting, bargains are now a rarity. The Antique Shop (146 Wen Tah Road; telephone: 34229) is an amalgamation of several smaller shops and caters exclusively to foreigners. A spacious center gallery has glass cases displaying jade, seals, and ink stones; its walls are decorated by scrolls. Two other rooms feature wooden carvings, screens, vases, and porcelains. The staff is helpful. The store has a certain orderliness that suggests nothing unusual is likely to be found there. The Antique Warehouse (Hung Shu Road) provides a less pleasant atmosphere for shopping, although its four back rooms house hundreds of items, some yet to be cleaned or prepared for sale (i.e., without the obligatory red wax seals certifying them for export).

During Fair times, antiques are sold in the arts and crafts section of the Light Industry Products Exhibition Hall. In 1976 there were reports of a new warehouse 20 km. outside of the city (in Cheung Pin Tsun Commune) specializing in items costing US$300 or more.

Shopping Tours

In addition to the specialty stores there are a variety of other shops concentrated in the two main shopping districts of Kwangchow: Peking Road and Ren Min Road.

☐ **Peking Road.** This area can be reached in a 30-minute walk from either the Bai Yun or Tung Fang hotels. The following excursion begins at the intersection of Peking Road and Chung Shan Road.

Street Number	Specialty
2	**Department Store.** Closed for renovations in late 1977, its selection rivals that of the Nan Fang (see Ren Min Road).
10	**Music Shop.** To the east of the department store (on the north side of the street), this is the largest musical shop in Kwangchow. A large drum can be had for Y30, a traditional Chinese lute for about Y35. Also available is a large selection of flutes (the membranes give Chinese flutes their distinctive "reedy" sound). *Wushu* (martial arts) paraphernalia are also sold here.
11	**Herbalist.** Crossing over to the south side, the aromas coming from this traditional herbal medicine store will pinpoint its location.
7	**Dress patterns.** Walking a few doors west (towards the intersection) this appears at first glance to be a dress and shirt shop, but its main feature is a large counter for sewing patterns.

Crossing over Peking Road and continuing east on Chung Shan Road (past the bank on the intersection) are the aquarium store (415) and the Cantonese sausage store (189).

393 **Decorative ornaments and housewares.** Signs in English advertising cloisonné and jade lead into a narrow store with counters flanking each side. By walking towards the back, up the stairs, past the bamboo furniture, and through the swinging doors, visitors come upon a small room for "foreigners only." There the staff serves tea while showing their wares.

Returning once again to the intersection, turn right (north) on Peking Road.

335 **Sporting goods.** A good selection, from ping-pong balls to warm-up outfits.

336 **Fu Wu Shih Tien Bookstore.** Specializing in technical books (all in Chinese).

344 **Taiping Restaurant.** The dining area for foreigners is a few flights up and to the back of the restaurant; portions are large.

363 **General merchandise.** Around the curve to the left, this store sells everything from door hinges to toilet paper. It is a good place to look for hand-made items such as brooms, baskets, crockery, and leather bags.

Returning once again to the intersection of Peking Road and Chung Shan Road, continue south. While looking at the stores, walkers should take note of the buildings and their roof-lines which present an interesting mélange of styles.

326 **Bookstore.** Specializes in political and ideological works.

322 **Art supplies.** Formally called the First Cultural and Antique Supplies Store, this shop also has a "back room" frequented by Japanese buyers looking for ink stones and Chinese brushes. It also sells scrolls.

319 **Hardware store.** In China, such stores carry everything from bicycle wheel rims (stacked high in the center of the floor) to television sets and radio parts.

314 **Poster shop.** One of the two places to buy political posters, an important mass art in China. Subjects include the calligraphy of Mao, the countenance of Hua Kuo-feng, anti-imperialist slogans, and diagrams teaching children how to brush their teeth.

303 **Beauty parlor.** The most "chic" in Kwangchow. The maximum charge is Y5 (US$2.65). No tipping.

301 **Stationery and school supplies.**

291 **Crockery.** Everyday cookware is quite attractive in China. One can buy sets as well as odd-lot pieces. The store also carries straw items, including hats (although peasant hats are ubiquitous in China, they are rarely sold through normal outlets; in the cities they are nearly impossible to find).

276 Bookstore. Specializes in high-school texts and literature.

273 Produce store. The most popular shop in the area for fresh fruit or a quenching soft drink (all fruit should be peeled before eating).

246 "General" store. This is as close to an "odd-lot" shop as one can find in China, with merchandise including used clothes, plastic flashlights, and pen knives.

☐ **Ren Min Road.** This commercial area, near the Pearl River, is popular among local people of the city as well as visitors from other parts of the country who can be seen buying maps and wandering around like tourists anywhere coming from the countryside to the city. Ren Min Road is a good 50-minute walk from the Tung Fang Hotel and is best reached by taxi. For the return trip, a taxi can be hired at the stand in front of 10-12 Ren Min Road. For the more adventurous, the three-wheeled vehicles available acrosss the street charge about half the rate of a regular taxi (they are not permitted to enter the gate of the hotel).

The tour starts at the Nan Fang Department Store which is just a few doors east of the Friendship Store, on the same side of the street (south).

36 Nan Fang Department Store. This is the largest retail outlet in Kwangchow. It's an ideal place to mix with the local people and get an idea of the range of commodities available in the local economy.

35 Dumpling Restaurant. Across the street from the Nan Fang, this is the most popular dumpling house in town; the system is to pay in advance for your order, collect a receipt, and hand it to the person serving from the huge wok.

Continue east a few steps to the intersection of Ren Min Road. This is a natural gathering place where "big-character posters" and slogans appear during political campaigns. The best way to explore Ren Min Road itself is to go up one side of the street and back down the other. Thus, starting on the west side and proceding north, there are:

9 Bookstore. This is a good place to buy a map of Kwangchow (8 fen). Although the legend is in Chinese, the street plan is clear and correlates easily with the map in this *Guide*.

While walking along the street, note the young girls and boys selling small items on the pavement—these range from hair pins to seasonal nuts and spices.

23   **Aquarium Store.** In China, aquarium stores sell not only fish, but plants, flowers, vases, and lanterns.

27   **Film Shop.** This place sells Kodak film (minus the canisters). A roll of C135-36 Kodacolor II costs Y2.30 (US$1.80).

47   **Bookstore.** Specializing in theoretical journals.

65   **Lantern Shop.** A good place to buy round Chinese lanterns, ranging in size from 6 in. to 6 ft. All are collapsible for easy packing.

Cross over to the east side and head south towards the river.

60   **Barber Shop.** Curiously resembling the set for a cowboy film with its swinging wooden doors, old chairs, and barber pole.

44   **Dried fruits.** A popular commodity in China, their taste is unmarred by chemical treatment.

Nanning

Nanning is the capital of Kwangsi Autonomous Region and is the southernmost of China's major cities. It lies some 300 mi. due west of Kwangchow and has a population of 350,000. Closed off to visitors until 1977, it is now being included in shorter itineraries that originate from Hong Kong (and include Kwangchow and Kweilin).

The town was founded during the Mongol Dynasty, serving as a market center on the trade routes that extended west to the Himalayan plateau and south to Annam (Vietnam) and elsewhere in southeast Asia. Nanning began to develop industrially in the 20th century and now has food-processing factories, flour mills, sugar refineries, tanneries, printing works, chemical fertilizer plants, and bauxite and coal mines. The predominant crops are rice and sugarcane. The region is also China's leading producer of tung oil.

There are few sites of major interest in the town other than a Drum Tower and a Bell Tower. In describing the city, Chinese publications note that it was an "important center during the Vietnam War"; i.e., it served as a major staging base for Soviet and Chinese war materiel and other assistance.

Kweilin

桂
林

cassia woods
Pinyin Spelling: Guilin ("gway-lin")

Approached by air, Kweilin's scenery suddenly changes from flat agricultural lands and rounded hills to a forest of sharp, jutting peaks set amidst the blue-gray of lakes and rivers. This, then, is the most famous scenic spot in China, long memorialized in painting and poetry. As the classical poet Han Yu described it: "The river forms a green gauze belt, the mountains are like blue jade hairpins." Kweilin is becoming increasingly accessible to visitors. Today, the whole area is prized not only for its scenery but also for its increasing role as a regional manufacturing center.

Kweilin is in a subtropical region of China, situated in the northeastern corner of Kwangsi Autonomous Region. In prehistoric times, the area was covered by an expanse of sea. The karst landscape was created by the erosion of the limestone surface, forming steep, isolated hills, caverns, and underground channels.

Kweilin has a population of 320,000, with the municipal area covering 780 sq.km. (300 sq.mi.). The urban center itself is only 160 sq.km. (60 sq.mi.). Kweilin is located on the west bank of the Li River and is a stop on the rail line between Nanning and Chaugsha, thus making it an important link in the transportation network of southern China. The subtropical climate results in long summers that are wet and hot. Spring and fall seasons are notably pleasant.

Kweilin in History

Kweilin was founded in 214 BC as a way-station on the Li River. It gained in importance when the emperor completed a two-and-a-half mile canal as part of a link between the Yangtse River in central China and the Pearl River to the south, thereby bypassing the arduous mountain trails. Today, the canal is used as an irrigation aqueduct. Under the Ming Dynasty, Kweilin was designated a provincial capital and remained so until 1914 (when it was superseded by Nanning). Kweilin was again named a capital in 1936 and, during the anti-Japanese war, it was a stronghold of resistance (the location of some caves were not discovered by the present government until the late 1950s). During the war, printing plants, newspapers, and theatrical companies took refuge here, and the population grew rapidly. Much of the city was heavily damaged or destroyed by bombing raids during this period.

Kweilin's most notable expansion took place after 1949. The city has since doubled its size, the industrial base growing from 4 factories to 260. Farming has been enhanced by the construction of some 2,000 water-control projects—reservoirs, ponds, and irrigation canals. Today the city is neatly laid out, with two- and three-storied stucco buildings replacing the blocks of older mud homes on the river banks. Each fall, hundreds of cassia trees (*osmanthus*)—planted during the last 20 years—fill the air with the fragrance of their yellow, white, and red blossoms. The trees yield tea, herbal medicine, fragrant oil, and a flavorful local wine.

Economy and Culture

In 1949, Kweilin had only one printing plant and a few small factories and handicrafts industries. Since then, numerous factories have been built and the city now employs a workforce of about 100,000. Kweilin produces nitrogen fertilizers, spun silk, cotton cloth, tires, medicines, rubber, machinery, and a wide range of other products. Machine-tool manufacturing gained prominently during the Cultural Revolution and today the city also produces electronic components, semiconductor apparatus, and transistor radios. Traditional commodities include wine, bean products, candy, pepper sauce, bamboo chopsticks, umbrellas, and perfumes.

The agricultural sector has also been expanded by means of planned development. Major products include grain, rice, bamboo, pomelos, persimmons, and cassia byproducts. Fishing is an important activity, as is river commerce.

HIGHLIGHTS FOR TRAVELERS

Time spent in Kweilin is invariably too short. The scenery is magnetic: the crags and rivers seem to take on a new aspect with every change in light. Clouds, sunlight, mist, and rain all have dramatic effects on the mood. Equally distinctive are the region's caves: the unearthly beauty of stalagtite and stalagmite formations rivals that of the surface.

Camel Mountain

☐ **Banyan Lake (Jung Hu).** Completely relandscaped in recent years, this lake is the focus of an attractive park with gardens, pavilions, and walkways. Under the T'ang Dynasty, the lake formed part of a moat that protected the town walls. It is now flanked by two hotels and a new city auditorium.

☐ **Seven Star Park (Chi Hsing Shan).** This park, located just across a bridge in the eastern section of the city, consists of a large expanse of lawns and cassia trees. Its most noted attraction is Seven Star Hill, whose peaks are arranged more or less in the shape of the Big Dipper (*Ursa Major*). The hill also contains six legendary caves. Their entrances are marked by steles and inscriptions dating from the T'ang, Sung, and Ming dynasties. A 1,000-meter-long path winds through the main cave, passing many stalagtite formations that have been floodlit in color and (with a little prompting from local guides) conjure up fruits, animals, and human figures.

☐ **Fu Po Hill.** This is probably the most interesting of the several hills situated within the city limits of Kweilin. The steps and walkways en route to the top are surrounded with interesting sights, among them an enormous cooking pot formerly used in a temple; a south-facing temple surrounded by viewing pavilions, and a cave with many famous engravings. The top of the hill affords a magnificent view in all directions. Taking a different way down, the visitor passes

Returned Pearl Cave. Here, legend has it, a fisherman once stole a gleaming pearl used by a dragon to light the cave, but he was so filled with shame that he returned it. Near the cave is Thousand Buddha Cliff, noted for over 300 statues, some dating from the T'ang and Sung dynasties. At the end of the visit, tea is served in a pavilion overlooking the river.

☐ **Reed Flute (Luti) Cave.** Of the many caves around the city, Reed Flute Cave (also known as Reed Pipe Cave) is the most famous. The reeds in question still grow at the cave entrance, and were used to make flutes as well as to conceal the opening. Thought to have been first discovered during the T'ang Dynasty (over 1,100 years ago), the cave became a frequent shelter for the local populace seeking to escape the ravages of wars and bandits. Since 1959, it has gradually been transformed into a tourist attraction. A trail extends 500 m. through the cave to an adjoining tea house that affords a grand panorama of mountains, farmland, and the distant Li River.

The chief attraction in the cave itself is its stalagtite formations which, with the aid of somewhat contrived colored spotlights, cast shadows that resemble everything from bumper harvests to a big-city skyline. Chickens and ferocious lions are all part of the internal landscape of Reed Flute Cave, whose stalagtites and stalagmites are still growing at a rate of one inch every 100 years.

☐ **Li River.** The highlight of a trip to Kweilin is the 6-hour, 50-mile journey down the winding Li River to Yangshou. Visitors are taken aboard a launch, which is pulled and poled over rapids and shallows and along crags, valleys, and bamboo groves. The excursion passes fishermen on bamboo rafts using trained cormorants—their necks tied to prevent swallowing all but the smallest fish. River craft traveling upstream are towed in a convoy by tugs. Some are still pulled by men and women in harnesses. Along the way, some of the famous rock formations passed include Elephant Trunk Hill—just outside Kweilin proper, this rock suggests an elephant drinking from the river; Lohona Rock—profile of a man with shaven head and long neck; Old Man Peak—trees and shrubs form eyebrows and whiskers on a man's face; Crown Hill—a colossal crown; Ram's Horn Hill; Painting Hill (also known as Nine Horse Hill)—the light has to be particularly good and the imagination vivid to see them all; Ehrlang Gorge; Brocade Hill—vegetation of different colors; Moon Hill (in Yangshou) this hill has a flat top with a cave—the shape of a half-moon.

Although Yangshou itself is a colorful and distinctive town, schedules do not permit a lingering look. The bus ride back takes about

The Li River

two hours and is equally spectacular, especially during rice harvesting season when the golden stalks, bathed in evening light, offer a sharp contrast to the black hills etched on the horizon.

WALKING TOURS

Because of its small size and well laid-out streets, Kweilin is an ideal city to explore on foot. The Kweilin Hotel looms nearly everywhere on the skyline, making it easy to check one's bearings. Using Banyan Lake Bridge as a base point (a spot equidistant from the Banyan Tree Lake Hotel and the Kweilin Hotel), walk south along the main road (leading out of town). There are some large stores here, including the best souvenir shop in the city (which functions in lieu of a Friendship Store). Further down the street, on the right, is an antiques store, with some items marked for foreigners and others exclusively for Chinese.

To the north of the bridge the main shopping district begins with the department store on the east side of the street. On the same side are some shops featuring cigarette-holders said to be good for (or less bad for?) asthma. A covered market area is one block west of the main street and runs parallel to it. To the east, one can walk along a section of an old palace wall (built in 1393) and among modern residential buildings. Walk up to Chieh Fang Road, the major east-west thoroughfare, until reaching the bridge (two blocks). Winding south again along the shaded river bank, the walkway returns the visitor to the Kweilin Hotel.

HOTEL ACCOMMODATIONS

Until 1976, only a few hundred visitors a year—mostly overseas Chinese—visited Kweilin. But now, with the completion of a 20-story hotel and the expansion of the airport, larger numbers can be accommodated.

☐ **Kweilin Hotel.** This hotel was completed in 1976 and dominates the center of the city. Guests on either side have an unrivaled view of the surrounding city and mountains. Services include a post office, bank, retail shop (with some excellent local crafts for sale), food store, and a large Western dining room. The hotel has steam heat and, in colder months, provides comforters. Even though superstitions are ostensibly eschewed in today's China, the number 13 does not appear on the premises.

☐ **Banyan Tree Lake Hotel.** Because of its size, this establishment falls more in the category of a guest house. It offers comparatively luxurious accommodations for visiting dignitaries and official delegations. A four-story structure with 100 rooms, its dining room serves many colorful local specialties, including rice birds and snake-bile wine.

SHOPPING

The best buys in Kweilin include local bamboo products (the plaited miniature suitcases make sturdy cosmetic cases or overnight bags), carved and painted stones, and local food specialties, including cassia wine, cassia tea, snake-bile wine (recognizable by its green-colored contents), fruit (oranges from Kwangsi provided the seed stock for California oranges). Another product known in the area is embroidered linens, available at very reasonable prices.

Changsha

long sandbank
Pinyin Spelling: Changsha (chong-shah)

Changsha, the capital of Hunan Province, is a flourishing regional center for culture and education. Situated in south-central China at the lower reaches of the Hsiang River, Changsha lies 525 km. (315 mi.) northwest of Kwangchow and 1,350 km. (810 mi.) south of Peking. It is one of three principal stops on the Peking-Kwangchow railway line (12 hours from Kwangchow, 26 from Peking). The greater municipality of Changsha has an area of 2,990 sq. km. (1,800 sq.mi.). The central city occupies about 110 sq.km. (66 sq.mi.) and supports a population of 800,000.

Physically, Changsha offers only modest historic and scenic attractions. It owes its significance to two factors: the intensively cultivated alluvial lowlands surrounding the city are among the most productive in China. And, not incidently, the city played a major role in the lives and political careers of both Mao Tse-tung and Hua Kuo-feng.

Mao was born in neighboring Shaoshan (discussed below) and attended high school in Changsha. His observations of life in this area served as the basis of the most important of his early political works, "Report on the Peasant Movement in Hunan Province." Prior to his appointment as Mao's successor in 1976, Chairman Hua Kuo-feng held important political and administrative posts in Hunan. An agricultural specialist, Hua helped direct much of the reclamation and irrigation work undertaken in the area during the past 15 years.

Changsha in History

The site of Changsha was inhabited as long as 3,000 years ago. Metallurgy, textile handicrafts, and lacquer work have flourished since the Spring and Autumn and Warring States periods (770-221 BC). Changsha was the site of a recently-excavated tomb dating from the Western Han period (206 BC-24 AD) containing some remarkable, superbly preserved artifacts.

Changsha was known as an important educational center as early as the Sung Dynasty (ca. 11th century AD). A large encircling wall with nine gates (portions of which are still standing) was built during the Ming period.

In 1904, an "open-door" treaty established Changsha as a foreign-trade port. Afterwards, large numbers of Europeans and Americans began to take up residence in the city. Foreign influences were soon manifested in the establishment of churches, educational institutions —including a college set up by Yale University (now a medical center), and a number of small export factories.

Mao Tse-tung lived in the city as a student from 1912-18. It was here that his conversion to communism began. Local guides relate that during this period Mao matured politically from a naive country lad who had never read a newspaper to a questioning student, progressive teacher, and local political organizer. One of his first jobs was editing the local *Hsiang River Review*. Many of the sites associated with those days are indispensable parts of the visitor's itinerary.

Changsha suffered acute damage during the Sino-Japanese War (1937-45), and much of it remained in ruins until after the establishment of the PRC in 1949. By 1952, reconstruction and rehabilitation were well underway and important initiatives in industrialization had begun.

Economy and Culture

Changsha served as a major trading center for more than 2,000 years. Prior to the 20th century, most commercial activity stemmed from agriculture. Hunan has traditionally been a surplus food producer, annually furnishing about 15% of China's total rice crop. At least a dozen rice mills are now in operation in Changsha and constitute the most important single economic activity in the city.

An early boost to development occurred when Changsha was linked by rail to Hankow and Peking in 1908, providing an impetus for the growth of modern light industry, particularly textiles and food processing. Today, although the city's economy is still strongly tied to its agricultural hinterland, the traditional dominance of food-processing and handling has significantly diminished. The trend toward economic diversification has featured the establishment of small and medium-sized machinery, chemical, electronics, and metal-working plants. A new railway terminus was completed in 1977.

River transportation remains another aspect of Changsha's economy. Although its cargo facilities have yet to be modernized, Changsha remains the busiest port on the Hsiang River. Food grains, construction materials, coal, and timber account for about 70% of the freight handled. Shipments arrive in long, graceful, flat-sailed cargo boats or on low-riding, utilitarian barges.

Culturally, Changsha is noted for its marionette and shadow-puppet theater. Recently, its museum has become a major attraction by virtue of the Han tomb excavation. (See below.) The city's major educational and cultural centers are located on the west bank of the river at the base of Yueh-lu Shan. These include Hunan University, Hunan Teachers College, and the Central-South Institute of Metallurgy. Changsha also boasts 13 hospitals and an Institute of Chinese Traditional Medicine.

HIGHLIGHTS FOR TRAVELERS

Changsha is a relatively new addition to the itinerary of visiting foreigners and, with the exception of the museum, there are few unique displays of Chinese antiquity, architecture, or other cultural attractions. Rather, it is the countryside and the sites associated with Chairman Mao and his early revolutionary activities that are the focal points for visitors.

□ **Hunan Provincial Museum.** The Provincial Museum, located in a large park in the northeast section of town (near the hotel), was formerly known mainly for its collection of documents dealing with revolutionary history. While the collection is still there, most attention now focuses on the relics unearthed from Han Tomb No. 1 at Mawangtui, a site just two miles east of the museum. The site, excavated in 1972, featured two spectacular finds: the first was the perfectly preserved corpse of a woman about 50 years old. She was apparently the wife of a royal personnage and had lived around 193-141 BC. Individual organs removed from her body are on display. Details of her life have been deduced from items found in her stomach and other medical evidence. The body itself is in the basement of the museum and may be viewed through a plexiglass skylight.

When found, the body was wrapped in more than 20 layers of silk and linen with a silk painting draped over the inner coffin. In three layers, it depicts scenes of the underworld, of human society, and of the celestial world. Some details derive from legend, others from the society of the time. The painting retains its brilliant colors, with figures outlined by a single flowing line and colored with mineral pigments of vermilion, azurite, and malachite. Other funerary objects on display from this tomb are the three lacquered coffins, gowns of silk gauze, lacquer ware, musical instruments, and some outstanding figurines.

□ **Lovely Evening Pavilion (Ai Wan).** Situated on Yue-lu Hill on the west bank of the Hsiang River, the Ai Wan Pavilion commands a striking view of the town. It is a popular place for the people of Shaoshan to relax and picnic in their time off. The pavilion itself has a double roof with glazed green tiles.

□ **Orange Island (Chieh-tzu Chou).** This island is in fact the "long sandbank" from which Changsha takes its name. Lying midstream in the Hsiang River, it runs almost the length of the city. The Orange Island Pavilion, at its southern tip, affords a commanding view of river traffic. The Hsiang River Bridge, at the island's northern end, was completed in the early 1970s. Before then, ferries were the only means of transport across the river.

□ **Museum at Hunan Normal School.** Mao Tse-tung attended classes here between 1913 and 1918, and later returned there to teach. Destroyed during the civil war, the school has been carefully restored to serve as a monument to Mao and the Chinese Revolution.

□ **Former Office of the Hunan Communist Party Committee.** This museum includes the rooms used for early meetings, Mao's living quarters, and an exhibition of historical materials from that period.

HOTEL ACCOMMODATIONS

☐ **Hunan Guest House.** The nine-story Hunan Guest House, built in 1959, is Changsha's tallest building and offers the city's best tourist accommodations. Located at the edge of the Martyrs Park (Lieh-shih Kuang-yuan) and about a mile and a half from the main square, it has over 250 rooms and can accommodate up to 600 people. A staff of 250 presides over this rather cavernous structure which, until the recent upsurge in tourism, had remained relatively empty. Services include three modern dining rooms, a souvenir shop, a crafts emporium, and other amenities such as barber and beauty shops, telephones, post office, bank, and laundry. The lobby has a map showing bus routes to other parts of the city. Rates are Y14-18 for a twin-bedded room; a suite is Y60.

Shaoshan

Shaoshan is located 131 km. (78 mi.) southwest of Changsha. It is accessible by motor coach (three hours) and train (rarely used by foreign visitors). The village is in Hsiangtan County and is so small it does not appear on many large-scale maps of China. Its importance in the history of the Communist movement, however, far surpasses its physical dimensions, as it is the birthplace of Mao Tse-tung.

The road to Shaoshan is well-paved and passes through some of the most verdant countryside in China. The distinctive styles of Hunan dress (the unique peasant hats, for example), carts, and architecture quickly become apparent.

Shaoshan itself is in a narrow valley surrounded by hills, the highest of which is the site of a Taoist hermitage. The main attractions, of course, are the birthplace of Mao Tse-tung and the Mao Tse-tung Museum. For overnight visitors, a walk through the surrounding countryside and the small village is recommended.

☐ **Mao Tse-tung Birthplace.** The house where Mao Tse-tung was born in 1893 will surprise many by its relatively large size. It contains three bedrooms (the third for Mao's brother, killed during the civil war), a spare guest room, rice granary, separate kitchen, adjoining bathroom, stable area, and sheds for cows, tools, and wood. Just in front of the house is a small pond with lotus flowers where Mao used to swim as a small boy. Nearby are the rice fields where he worked. (Everything is duly noted by signs in Chinese and English.)

Mao's birthplace, Shaoshan

☐ **Mao Tse-tung Museum.** Opened in 1967, the museum focuses on Mao's early childhood and his revolutionary activities spanning the three decades between 1920 and 1950. The museum's circumspect planners built two wings that exactly duplicate each other, picture for picture, so as to better accommodate the large crowds of visitors (foreign and Chinese).

HOTEL ACCOMMODATIONS

☐ **Shaoshan Guest House.** Although Shaoshan can be seen during a day's outing from Changsha, some tours may be housed overnight at this spartan but comfortable hotel. The furniture is simple and the floors are unrelieved concrete and terrazo. Its two main buildings overlook the town, only minutes away on foot. The main building has a dining room, lecture halls, retail shop, and a ping-pong table—the scene of many friendly matches (or, more commonly, mis-matches) between visitors and their adept Chinese guides. The main sleeping quarters for foreigners are in a separate building to the rear.

HUNAN CUISINE

Although Hunan is a province noted for its spicy, flavorful food, this feature may elude tourists whose meals are confined to the hotel's dining room. Apparently, the hotel is under instructions to refrain from challenging their guests' palates and, as a result, blander versions of

Hunan fare are the rule. The alert tour group will try to make a special request of the kitchen or try to negotiate an evening at a local restaurant with the tour guides (Shaoshan has no restaurants catering to foreigners, although the open hospitality of the local people may afford a chance to try the simple fare of a local restaurant). Vegetables prepared with special local sauces, and any of the "spicy" dishes offered will quickly reveal why Hunan's food has gained such a wide reputation. The region is also famous for its oranges and kumquats.

SHOPPING

The people of Changsha and Shaoshan produce an array of distinct regional handicrafts. The embroidery is justly famous. Hotel shops display crafts such as miniature sampans made from shells. Pottery and ceramic ware is also recommended (especially the tiny figurines) as are eiderdowns (quilts and pillows filled with duck feathers). Shaoshan offers a variety of Mao Tse-tung memorabilia, including lapel buttons made of lacquered bamboo.

The Chinese Export Commodities Fair

"Canton Trade Fair"

Negotiations in the Exhibition Hall

The Kwangchow (Canton) Trade Fair, held twice yearly in the spring and fall, is the most important event in the Chinese business calendar. Officially known as the Chinese Export Commodities Fair, it accounts for nearly half of China's yearly export sales and about a third of the country's total trade turnover. China's total trade was estimated at US$14 billion in 1977, placing it 35th among the world's trading nations.

The first Kwangchow Fair was held in October 1957, when 1,200 visitors from 20 countries and regions came to the Kwangtung Provincial Exhibition Hall on Pearl River Square to view some 12,000 products. The Fair has been held twice a year ever since, in the spring from April 15 to May 15, and in the fall from October 15 to November 15. The 1978 Fairs were the 43rd and 44th, respectively.

The Fair has gradually grown in size and importance, although business declined somewhat during the Cultural Revolution period (1966-68) when, to use the Chinese phrase, politics took command. Since then, the pace of business has again picked up. A new Fair complex, more than twice the size of the original, opened in April 1974. The new complex covers 60,000 square meters of exhibition space, divided among 12 exhibition halls. Some 40,000 items were on display in the mid-1970s, and each Fair was attracting over 25,000 visitors from 150 countries and regions.

Attendance by US businessmen at the Fairs began in spring 1972 when a dozen were invited. The Fall 1977 Fair was attended by some 700 Americans, representing 300 companies—the second largest contingent, after Japan. Official representation by Canadian businessmen began in 1971, a year after the establishment of full diplomatic ties between Canada and the PRC. The Fall 1977 Fair was attended by 75 Canadian representatives.

Chinese officials at the Fair represent nine of China's Foreign Trade Corporations, dealing in the general areas of cereals, oils, and foodstuffs; native products and animal by-products; textiles; light industrial goods; chemicals; metals and minerals; machinery; and handicrafts (for which an independent trade corporation was established in January 1978).

Unlike other international trade fairs, the Kwangchow Fair is designed to be a showcase of current Chinese export potential and industrial development as well as a venue for direct business negotiations. Thus, it is a "permanent" exhibition and, as the official title suggests, it is a place mainly used for negotiating Chinese export business. Foreign companies may not acquire display space.

As China's goods have found increased acceptance in world markets, prices have kept pace, and there are few "bargains" to be had. Standards of quality remain high and the Chinese have shown increased flexibility with regard to packaging and design. The most often heard lament is product-availability and price; nevertheless, business continues to be brisk.

During 1976, a re-evaluation of the Fair's role in China's export trade seems to have taken place, and a series of mini-fairs are now held in other parts of China for specific products (e.g., the Peking Carpet Fair held in February 1978).

GETTING TO THE FAIR

Fair Invitations

Attendance at the Kwangchow Trade Fair is by invitation only. As a rule, invitations are first sent to those foreign corporations that have established trade ties with China. Invitations are generally issued by one of China's nine state trading corporations, headquartered in Peking, whose product lines roughly define the range of commodities that China seeks to export.

Firms seeking to initiate business with China should first write to the Peking headquarters of the appropriate PRC trade corporation. Under some circumstances, invitations to the Fair may be solicited by writing directly to the Chinese Export Commodities Fair, Pearl River Square, Kwangchow, People's Republic of China; to the PRC Liaison Office (2300 Connecticut Avenue N.W., Washington, D.C. 20008) or other overseas PRC embassies; to the Commercial Attaché, Embassy of the PRC (for residents of eastern Canada), 415 St. Andrews Street, Ottawa, Ontario K1N 5H3; to the Consular Office of the PRC (for residents of western Canada), 500 West 12th Avenue, Vancouver, British Columbia V5Z 1M2; or to the China Resources Company in Hong Kong.

Requests for an invitation should take the form of a letter of introduction and should include detailed information on the company's history, product lines, and sales volume. Bank references, financial reports, Dun and Bradstreet ratings, and other supporting data should be included. Requests for an invitation should precede the Fair opening by 2-3 months.

Holders of invitations are permitted to have a maximum of three representatives accompany them to China. The party may include spouses.

HEAD OFFICES OF CHINA'S FOREIGN TRADE CORPORATIONS

China National Arts and Crafts Import and Export Corporation

82 Tung An Men, Peking, People's Republic of China
Cable: ARTCHINA PEKING

China National Chemicals Import and Export Corporation

Erh Li Kou, Hsi Chiao, Peking, People's Republic of China
Cable: SINOCHEM PEKING

China National Native Produce and Animal By-Products Corporation

82 Tung An Men, Peking, People's Republic of China
Cable: CHINATUHSU PEKING

China National Light Industrial Products Import and Export Corporation

82 Tung An Men, Peking, People's Republic of China
Cable: INDUSTRY PEKING

China National Textiles Import and Export Corporation

82 Tung An Men, Peking, People's Republic of China
Cable: CHINATEX PEKING

China National Cereals, Oils and Foodstuffs Import and Export Corporation

82 Tung An Men, Peking, People's Republic of China
Cable: CEROILFOOD PEKING

China National Machinery Import and Export Corporation

Erh Li Kou, Hsi Chiao, Peking, People's Republic of China
Cable: MACHIMPEX PEKING

China National Metals and Minerals Import and Export Corporation

Erh Li Kou, Hsi Chiao, Peking, People's Republic of China
Cable: MINMETALS PEKING

China National Technical Import Corporation

Erh Li Kou, Hsi Chiao, Peking, People's Republic of China
Cable: TECHIMPORT PEKING

Visas

Once an invitation to the Fair is received, the prospective visitor must apply for PRC entrance and exit visas. Standard visas are for 35 days and are valid for Kwangchow only. They are not renewable, although they may be extended should negotiations in China so require. Many transactions at the Fair, however, can be conducted within 5-10 days. In the US, visa application forms can be obtained from the PRC office in Washington. In Canada, visa forms can be obtained from the PRC Embassy in Ottawa or the Consular Office in Vancouver. Others may make requests from the official China Travel Service (HK) Ltd. (37 Queen's Road Central, Hong Kong), or from PRC embassies or diplomatic posts elsewhere. Visa forms should be submitted in duplicate, together with the applicant's passport, two passport photos, and a processing fee ($6.00 for US citizens). Passports are usually returned with a visa stamp in one week.

Climate

Kwangchow has a subtropical climate, with warm, humid weather throughout most of the year. During the Spring Fair, temperatures range from a maximum of 84°F to a minimum of 65°F, with humidity averaging 74%. The autumn temperature range is 67°-85°F, with lower humidity—about 52%.

Time

Eastern Standard Time is 13 hours behind Kwangchow time. Thus, 8 PM in Kwangchow is 7AM of the same day in New York and Toronto.

Useful Items to Take Along

For the businessman, an ample supply of business cards is an important asset at the Fair. Bilingual cards (in English and Chinese) can be ordered in Hong Kong, at the Fair, or through Japan Air Lines' Executive Services. Other items that may prove useful include high-wattage light bulbs for the hotel room, a portable radio, and a typewriter. Current in Kwanchow is 220 volts, 50 cycles.

DOING BUSINESS AT THE FAIR

Advance Preparations and Contacts

Advance preparation is essential to the conduct of successful business negotiations at the Fair. Although political and cultural differences

DIAGRAM OF THE TRADE FAIR
EXHIBITION HALL

between Chinese trade representatives and Western businessmen are not overt aspects of the negotiation process, the tone of the relationship and how it develops will often govern Chinese attitudes on who they will do business with, on how much business will be done, and on what is traded.

There is no attempt at the "hard sell" in China. On the contrary, the passive attitude of the Chinese trade representatives, who behave more like order-takers than salesmen, has been noted by many. It is important, therefore, to form as clear an idea as possible beforehand about the nature and quantity of the purchase being sought. The wide variety of products on display will tempt window-shopping. An impulsive decision can be counter-productive, however, since it may then take two or three days simply to find the appropriate Chinese representative to discuss the product and its availability.

Further, it is important to arrive prepared with the detailed specifications required, not only to save time in communicating back and forth with the home office, but also to be able to fill in specific entries in the contract. Knowledge of current pricing levels, whether they be for shoes or chemicals, is also important. Buyers will find the Chinese to be very much abreast of world market conditions.

Due consideration should be given to the choice of a company's representative to be sent to the Fair. It is vital—in the Chinese view—that representatives have the authority to sign contracts. They should have a good working knowledge of the product areas to be explored. There is an advantage to having continuity of representation from Fair to Fair, since this will help promote an "old friend" relationship with Chinese negotiators. The Chinese try to discourage "non-serious" buyers, namely those who pose as businessmen in order to see something of China, those who seek to sign only token orders on behalf of a company, or those who come merely to browse.

Finally, it is necessary to set realistic goals about how much business can be done. It takes 3-5 days to do in China what can be done in 1-2 days elsewhere in Asia or the West. The Chinese are extremely cautious and meticulous in their dealings, and the extra time required to come to terms on prices, delivery, quantity, and specifications can place unneeded pressures on a hurried businessman. Patience is the rule. Learning the ropes about doing business at the Fair has become easier due to the several years' experience gained by a host of Western traders, including agents and trade representatives. The Chinese themselves publish guides to the Fair, and a helpful magazine called *China's Foreign Trade* is available from the PRC

Liaison Office in Washington or directly from China Publications Center (*Guozi Shudian*), P.O. Box 399, Peking. A basic source in the US for information on the China market is the National Council for US-China Trade (1050 17th Street N.W., Washington, D.C. 20036). The Council holds Fair briefings, publishes a bi-monthly trade magazine (*The China Business Review*), and maintains a knowledgeable staff. In Canada, information is available from the China Desk, Asia Division, Federal Government Department of Industry, Trade, and Commerce, 240 Queen Street, Ottawa, Ontario K1A OH4; tel: (613) 992-9386.

The Negotiation Process

China's negotiators at the Fair are representatives of the state-owned foreign trade corporations—they are not consumers, end-users, manufacturers, or suppliers. Nevertheless, these personnel are well versed in their assigned product areas.

First Contacts. Business hours at the Fair are 8:30-11:30 AM and 2:30-5:30 PM daily (except Sundays). It is necessary to go directly to the section of the Exhibition Hall featuring products of interest to the foreign buyer (see Exhibition Hall Diagram), and to seek out the appropriate Chinese officials in order to set up an appointment. A business card should be presented. Because of the large number of visitors to the Fair, appointments should be secured as soon as possible. In no case, however, can they be made prior to arrival in Kwangchow. Appointment times can be set in person or through a third party such as the Fair Liaison Office at the hotel. Arriving late or missing an appointment is considered rude, and broken appointments will be difficult to reschedule.

The Style of Negotiations. Business negotiations may take place in individual discussion rooms or, frequently, in corridors or the exhibition halls themselves. It is not unusual to find competitors sitting at directly adjacent tables. There may be 3-4 Chinese negotiators present, some of whom may abruptly get up and leave, while others randomly wander in, perhaps interrupting the train of conversation. Such procedures are considered normal practice, and it is important to retain aplomb.

Export Negotiations. The Kwangchow Fair is largely geared toward importers, but exporters will sometimes be invited and given an opportunity to hold some initial discussions. Export negotiations at the Fair are usually exploratory in nature. Provided there is sufficient interest, the talks will usually move on to Peking for further discussion.

Contracts

The drawing-up of a contract concludes the negotiating process. The Chinese attach great importance to the contract stage, and assume strict compliance by all parties. Contract terms and conditions vary among foreign trade corporations and also according to the commodity being traded. It is important to specify in the contract all terms and conditions verbally agreed to during the negotiations. (Importers will also find it useful to repeat such stipulations when opening Letters of Credit.)

Standard features of Chinese contracts include requirements for import and export documentation, claims settlement, arbitration, insurance, and arrangements for inspection. Buyers of Chinese products are usually required to open an irrevocable Letter of Credit—payable to the Bank of China. The BOC has established correspondent relationships with banks and many countries, including the Canadian Imperial Bank of Commerce and the First National Bank of Chicago. Chinese trade was formerly negotiated in British sterling, but other major currencies—including the French franc, Swiss franc, Deutschemark, Belgian franc, Dutch guilder, and US dollar—have also become acceptable.

Shipping. For importers, the terms of the contract usually specify C+F or CIF. The PRC operates a large merchant fleet, much of it under charter, and has shown a strong preference for making its own shipping arrangements, with Hong Kong and Tokyo the most common transshipment points for the US. Goods destined for many Latin American and Canadian ports are shipped direct from the PRC, or in some cases, via Hong Kong.

Insurance. Chinese insurance coverage for CIF shipments is regulated through the Ocean Marine Cargo and Ocean Marine Cargo War Clauses of the People's Insurance Company of China. Many importers now prefer CIF to C+F terms, having found Chinese insurance a good value. China retains agents in most major international ports to handle claims.

Arbitration. Arbitration clauses in standard Chinese contracts generally call for negotiations in Peking under terms set by the Chinese Foreign Trade Arbitration Committee. In actual practice, however, arbitration proceedings are found to be cumbersome and the Chinese discourage them, preferring "friendly discussion" between the parties.

THE TRAVELER'S VOCABULARY

Chinese pronunciation (putunghua) *follows English word or phrase.*

GENERAL

I, me, mine: waw; waw-duh
we, us: waw-muhn
you; your: nee; nee-duh
he, she, it; his, hers, its: tah; tah-duh
them; their: tah-muhn; tah-muhn-duh
Hello, how are you?: nee how; nee how mah?
Goodbye: dzy jee-an
Good morning: dzow (or) dzow-ahn
Good evening: whahn ahn
Please . . . : ching
Thank you; many thanks: shee-eh shee-eh; daw shee-eh
What is your name?: ching-one gway shing
My name is . . . : waw da ming-tzuh shir . . .
I am . . . : waw shir
  American: may-gwo run
  British: ying-gwo run
  French: fah-gwo run
  Canadian: jah-nah-dah run

Japanese: ur-bun run
I don't understand: waw boo dung
I'm sorry: dway boo chee
When is . . . : summah shir hoe . . .
Where?: summah dee fahng (or) . . . tzy nah-lee
Who?: shay
Yes; correct; I agree: shir
don't agree: boo tung-ee
friend: pung yo
friendship: yo-ee
friendly: huh-chee
No thank you, I . . . : shee-eh shee-eh, waw . . .
  am unable to: boo-nung
  don't want . . . : boo-yow
  don't like . . . : boo shee-wahn
good; very good: how; huhn how
pleased; happy: hwahn–shee; kwy-luh
not good: boo-how

TRAVEL

airport: fay-jee tsahng
train station: whaw-tsuh tsahng
luggage: shing-lee
customs: high-swahn
car: chee chuh

bus: gung-gung chee-chuh
taxi: chee tsung chee-chuh
left: dzwaw
right: yo

SHOPPING

Where can I buy . . . : my-le . . . dzy nah lee
antiques: goo-dye
handicrafts: show-ee
art works: ee shu; goong

books: shoo
stamps: yo-beeow
department store: soong tee-en
How much is it?: daw shau chee-en

HEALTH

I don't feel well.: waw boo soo foo
I am ill.: waw yo bing
Please call a doctor.: ching ee-shung lee-eh
hospital: ee yu-ahn
dentist: yah-ee
aspirin: tsir tung yau
medicine: yau

pharmacy: yau tang
stomach pains: way toong
diarrhea: syeh-doo
I have a cold.: waw sahng fung-lah
headache: toe tung
It hurts here.: waw tsuh lee tung
Where can I get medical treatment?: nah-lee yo lee-ow?

HOTEL

hotel: lew kwahn
room: fahng jee-an
telephone: dee-an wah
toilet: tse-swo
light: dee-an
bath: shee-dzau

water: shway
Please come in!: ching chin lye
Wait a moment.: dung-ee-dung
key: ye-ow
laundry: shee-ee dee-an

DINING

restaurant: fahn gwahn
breakfast: tzau-chahn
lunch: woo-chahn
dinner: jeng-chahn

snack: dee-an shin
Cheers!: gahm bay
chopsticks: kwy-dzu
spoon: tahng-shir

What is your speciality?: summah tuh be-eh dah how tsy

I've had enough to eat: chir bow-luh

The food was delicious!: tsy how jee-lah

FOOD

beef: nee-oe
beer: pee-joe
chicken: jee
duck: yah-dzuh
eggs: chee dahn
fruit: shway gwoh
fish: yew
pork: joo-row
rice: fahn

shrimp: shah
soup: tahng
spicy: lah
tea: tsah
vegetable: ching tsy
water (cold): lee-ahng-duh
  shway
Western food: shee tsahn

SIGHTSEEING

We'd like to visit . . .: wawmun ye-ow chew . . .

factory: koong tsahng
museum: bwo woo gwan
park: gung yu-ahn

school: shoo-eh she-ow
store: song dee-en
take a picture: jau see-ahng

TIME, DATES, NUMBERS

(number) o'clock: . . . dee-an
  jong
What time is it?: jee dee-an
  joong
today: jin tee-an
tomorrow: ming tee-an
yesterday: dzoo-aw tee-an
year: nee-en
month: you-eh
one: ee
two: are
three: sahn
four: suh

five: woo
six: lee-oh
seven: chee
eight: bah
nine: chee-oh
ten: shir
eleven: shir-ee
twelve: shir-are
twenty: are-shir
thirty: sahn-shir
one hundred: ee bye
one thousand: ee chee-an

A CHINA-TRAVEL READING LIST

The list that follows seeks to provide a sampling of general works on the People's Republic of China. A more comprehensive bibliography can be found in Arlene Posner and Arne J. de Keijzer (eds.), *China: A Resource and Curriculum Guide* (Second edition, revised. Chicago: University of Chicago Press, 1976). A variety of bibliographies and background materials on China are available free or at very low cost from China-friendship organizations (see list, pp. 8-9). A number of bookstores also specialize in China materials (e.g., Books New China in New York; China Books and Periodicals in New York, Chicago, and San Francisco; and China Arts and Crafts in Vancouver).

Background

China Council of the Asia Society (comp.). *People's Republic of China: Press Briefing Materials*. Revised edition. New York: Learning Resources in International Studies, 1976. Originally prepared for President Ford's visit in 1975. Concise data, particularly on political background.

Cohen, Jerome and Joan. *China Today and Her Ancient Treasures*. New York: Harry N. Abrams, 1974. An excellent visual introduction to China's past and present.

Committee of Concerned Asian Scholars. *China! Inside the People's Republic*. New York: Bantam, 1972.

Coye, Molly Joe and Jon Livingston. *China Yesterday and Today*. New York: Bantam, 1975. An inexpensive (US$1.95) compendium of readings, documents, and observations.

Fairbank, John King. *The United States and China*. Third revised edition. Cambridge: Harvard University Press, 1972.

Gamberg, Ruth. *Red and Expert: Education in the People's Republic of China*. New York: Schocken, 1978.

Hinton, William. *Fanshen: A Documentary of a Revolution in a Chinese Village*. New York: Vintage, 1966. An absorbing, intimate account of the revolutionary transformation of a farming village in Shansi Province.

Kaplan, Fredric M., Julian M. Sobin, and Stephen Andors. *Encyclopedia of China Today*. New York: Eurasia Press and Harper & Row, 1978. A comprehensive single-volume reference work focusing on the post-1949 period.

Kessen, William, ed. *Childhood in China*. New Haven: Yale University Press, 1974. First-hand encounters between US educators and teachers, pupils, and parents in China.

Milton, David, and Nancy Dall Milton. *The Wind Will Not Subside: Years in Revolutionary China, 1964-1969*. New York: Pantheon, 1976. A first-hand account of the Cultural Revolution during 1964-69 by two resident teachers from the US.

Nagel's Encyclopedia Guide to China. Anne L. Destenay (trans.). Geneva, Switzerland: Nagel Publishers, 1974. Exhaustive descriptive information, especially on cultural aspects.

Newnham, Richard. *About Chinese*. Baltimore, Md. and Hammondsworth, England: Penguin, 1973. A readable introduction to the workings of the Chinese language.

Oksenberg, Michel, and Robert B. Oxnam. *China and America—Past and Future*. New York: Foreign Policy Association, 1977.

Schell, Orville. *In the People's Republic: An American's First-Hand View of Living and Working in China*. New York: Random House, 1977. The personal account of a China scholar's two-month experiences working in a PRC community and factory.

Schram, Stuart. *Mao Tse-tung*. New York: Pelican, 1967. A standard Western biography.

Sidel, Victor and Ruth. *Serve the People: Observations on Medicine in the People's Republic of China*. New York: Josiah J. Macy Foundation, 1973.

Snow, Edgar. *Red Star Over China*. New York: Vintage Books, 1971. Based on Snow's personal interviews with Mao and others in 1938, this is probably the most evocative first-hand account of the Chinese Communist movement in the period following the Long March.

Terrill, Ross. *800,000,000: The Real China*. New York: Laurel Press, 1972. Measured observations of Chinese life and politics, based on a visit by an Australian journalist now teaching at Harvard.

———*Flowers on an Iron Tree: Five Cities of China*. Boston: Little, Brown, 1975. Vivid descriptions of Shanghai, Talien, Hangchow, Wuhan, and Peking.

Tregear, Thomas R. *The Chinese: How They Live and Work*. London: Christopher Hurst, 1973. Daily life in the PRC.

Books From China

Most foreign-language titles from China are published by the Foreign Languages Press in Peking. They are available from bookstores specializing in PRC materials, or may be ordered from China Publications Center, P.O. Box 399, Peking. Most of the titles listed below are available in Spanish and French, as well as other languages.

Alley, Rewi. *Travels in China, 1966-1971*. 1973. Informal, wide-ranging narrative by a New Zealander long resident in China.

China—A Geographical Sketch. 1974. A basic introduction to China's principal geographical features.

China Travel Guide. 1975. Contains street maps for 27 cities on the traveler's itinerary.

A Glance at China's Culture. 1975. Includes medicine, science, education, and sports, as well as literature and art.

A Glance at China's Economy. 1974. A brief narrative survey.

Lu Hsun. *Selected Stories of Lu Hsun*. 1972. A collection of 18 short stories by China's most prominent revolutionary writer.

Mao Tse-tung. *Four Essays on Philosophy*. 1968.

———*Mao Tse-tung Poems*. 1976. 39 poems that span the revolutionary period.

———*On the Ten Major Relationships*. 1977. Essays on China's economic and social development.

———*Quotations From Chairman Mao Tse-tung*. 1972. Mao's "little red book," first published in 1966 as the handbook of the Red Guards.

———*Selected Works of Mao Tse-tung*. Vols. I-V. 1961-77. Official translation of Mao's writings, spanning the 1926-57 period.

———*Talks at the Yenan Forum on Literature and Art*. 1967. An important commentary on the relationship between art and politics in China.

Tachai—The Red Banner. 1977. A detailed history of the brigade's development since 1949.

Wu Ching-tzu. *The Scholars*. An 18th-century satirical novel still read in China.

Periodicals

Peking Review, a weekly publication from China, offers a good means of keeping abreast of official PRC views on domestic and international developments. Two illustrated PRC publications intended for general audiences are *China Reconstructs* (monthly) and *China Pictorial* (quarterly). Periodicals published outside of China include *New China*, a colorful, general-interest magazine produced by the US-China Peoples Friendship Association; *The China Quarterly*, and authoritative scholarly journal published in the UK; *Far Eastern Economic Review*, a Hong Kong weekly covering current political and economic developments; and *China Business Review*, an in-depth bimonthly publication of the National Council On US-China Trade.

INDEX

THE AUTHORS

Arne J. de Keijzer is founder of A. J. de Keijzer & Associates, Inc., a consulting firm specializing in the development of trade between the United States and the People's Republic of China. He was previously New York representative for the National Council for US-China Trade. Mr. de Keijzer has been involved in the opening of relations between the US and China since the days of "ping-pong diplomacy," having served for seven years on the staff of the National Committee on US-China Relations. Since 1978, he has visited China nine times. He is co-editor of *China: A Resource and Curriculum Guide* (University of Chicago Press, 1976) and is the author of a number of articles on US-China trade.

Fredric M. Kaplan is founder and publisher of Eurasia Press and former Executive Editor of *Worldmark Encyclopedia of the Nations*. A long-time specialist on China, he is co-author of *Encyclopedia Of China Today* (Harper & Row and Eurasia Press, 1978) and is Co-Chairperson of the US-China Peoples Friendship Association (New York).

Photo Credits

Katherine Smalley—p. 4; New China News Agency—pp. 17, 37, 50, 94, 98, 104, 152; National Council for US-China Trade—pp. 101, 172, 193; New China Magazine, p. 142. Graphic art from the People's Republic of China.